THE HUMAN PREDICAMENT

THE HUMAN PREDICAMENT

A Candid Guide to Life's Biggest Questions

David Benatar

OXFORD
UNIVERSITY PRESS

Oxford University Press is a department of the University of Oxford. It furthers
the University's objective of excellence in research, scholarship, and education
by publishing worldwide. Oxford is a registered trademark of Oxford University
Press in the UK and certain other countries.

Published in the United States of America by Oxford University Press
198 Madison Avenue, New York, NY 10016, United States of America.

Library of Congress Cataloging-in-Publication Data
Names: Benatar, David, author.
Title: The human predicament : a candid guide to life's biggest questions /
    by David Benatar.
Description: New York : Oxford University Press, 2017.
Identifiers: LCCN 2016048629 | ISBN 9780190633813 (hardcover : alk. paper)
Subjects: LCSH: Life. | Meaning (Philosophy)
Classification: LCC BD435 .B44 2017 | DDC 128—dc23
LC record available at https://lccn.loc.gov/2016048629

9 8 7 6

Printed by Sheridan Books, Inc., United States of America

To family and friends, who palliate my predicament.

CONTENTS

PREFACE

We are born, we live, we suffer along the way, and then we die—obliterated for the rest of eternity. Our existence is but a blip in cosmic time and space. It is not surprising that so many people ask: "What is it all about?"

The right answer, I argue in this book, is "ultimately nothing." Despite some limited consolations, the human condition is in fact a tragic predicament from which none of us can escape, for the predicament consists not merely in life but also in death.

It should come as no surprise that this is an unpopular view to which there will be considerable resistance. Thus, I ask my readers to keep an open mind while they read the arguments for my (generally though not entirely) bleak view. The truth is often ugly. (For some light relief, see the occasional joke or quip in the notes.)

Some readers may wonder what the relationship is between this book and my previous book (*Better Never to Have Been*[1]) in which I argued for other grim views—that coming into existence is a serious harm, and the anti-natalist conclusion that we ought not to create new beings. The first part of the answer is that, although the earlier book mentioned some of the topics covered in *The Human Predicament*, it did not discuss them in any depth.

The one point of significant overlap between the earlier book and the current one is that both discuss the poor quality of human life. Because I had examined that in some detail in *Better*

Never to Have Been, I did consider omitting it entirely from *The Human Predicament*. However, the quality of life is so much a part of the human predicament that forgoing any examination of it seemed like an egregious omission. That said, the arguments have been developed since I first presented them in *Better Never to Have Been*. I wrote about them afresh in chapter 3 of *Debating Procreation*[2] and then adapted that chapter for inclusion in *The Human Predicament*.

While the subject matters of *Better Never to Have Been* and *The Human Predicament* are very different, and while the arguments in the latter do not presuppose anti-natalism, they do provide further support for that view.

Although I have been working for many years on the themes covered in this volume, a draft of the book was written while I was a visiting scholar in the Bioethics Department at the National Institutes of Health (NIH), in Bethesda, Maryland. I am required to state—which I do with some amusement, because it is difficult in this case to imagine the confusion—that "the views expressed are those of the author and do not necessarily reflect those of the Clinical Center, the National Institutes of Health, or the Department of Health and Human Services."

It is my *pleasure* to add my thanks to the Bioethics Department for sponsoring my visit and for welcoming me for the stimulating academic year (2014–2015) I spent there. The theme of the Bioethics Department's Joint Bioethics Colloquium in the spring semester was "death," a happy coincidence about an unhappy topic. I benefited from discussions there and in a similarly themed reading group. At the NIH, I received helpful feedback on two chapters of the book. One of those chapters was also presented at both a brown bag seminar in the Philosophy Department at

George Washington University and a seminar in the Philosophy Department at the University of Cape Town. A paper adapted from one of the chapters was presented at a conference of the International Association for the Philosophy of Death and Dying in Syracuse, New York.

For helpful comments, I am grateful to participants in these forums. Special thanks to Joseph Millum and David Wasserman, who provided detailed written feedback on one chapter; to Travis Timmerman and Frederik Kaufman for written comments on the paper I presented at the conference on death and dying; and to David DeGrazia and Rivka Weinberg, who read and commented on the entire manuscript.

Jessica du Toit constructed the bibliography from my end-notes and converted all the references to the required style, meticulously detecting and correcting some errors in the process.

My thanks are also owed to the University of Cape Town for granting me the leave that enabled me to take up the visiting position at the National Institutes of Health and thus to write the book. I am also grateful to Peter Ohlin at Oxford University Press for his interest in the book and his helpful comments.

Finally, I extend my thanks to family and friends. They share the human predicament but meliorate mine. This book is dedicated to them.

D.B.

Cape Town

August 14, 2016

A READER'S GUIDE

The big existential questions may be thought to be the bread and butter of philosophers. Indeed, many philosophers, along with writers, artists, and others, have grappled with them. However, most of those philosophers who have examined these issues in ways that engage public interest have been philosophers from the (European) "continental" tradition. Think here of the French and German existentialists. Their style of writing is often more literary and evocative. While it has widespread appeal, analytic philosophers, who are more common in the Anglophone world, have often criticized this writing for being excessively obscure and insufficiently precise.

Analytic philosophers are—or at least profess to be—interested in rigorous arguments in which key terms are explicated, distinctions are drawn, and conclusions are validly inferred from premises. I agree that this sort of methodology is the path to wisdom in these and other matters. However, many—but by no means all, or even most—of those analytic philosophers who have engaged life's big questions have eviscerated these questions by descending into dry and arcane discussions about them. Readers fascinated by the questions are rapidly reduced to boredom.

Admittedly, it is difficult to navigate the correct path—a path that avoids the obscurantism of excessive rhetorical flourish and grand but imprecise pronouncements, but that also avoids abstruse, dull, hairsplitting analysis. In other words, it is not easy to present an accessible, engaging, and rigorous discussion of complex issues.

This book is not a work of popular philosophy. It is not written in the sort of popular style that appeals to mass audiences, and the views it defends are hardly likely to be popular, for reasons yet to be explained. (In the latter regard, I suppose that one might describe this book as a work of *unpopular* philosophy.) However, it has been written with the goal of being accessible and readable to intelligent lay readers and yet sufficiently rigorous to satisfy the professional (and aspiring professional) philosophers who constitute the other component of the book's intended readership. I can only hope that I have struck the right balance.

However, to assist those who may have less patience with the relatively technical and pedantic parts of the book, I provide here a guide to an abbreviated reading.

Chapter 1: Introduction

This short chapter should be an easy read for all. However, the first and last sections will have the broadest interest. Those readers who are less concerned about understanding some nuances of the nature of pessimism and optimism could skip the section entitled "Pessimism and optimism." The subsequent section ("The human predicament and the animal predicament") explains why I focus on the human predicament rather than the animal predicament more generally and may be skipped by those who do not need persuading.

Chapter 2: Meaning

The introduction to this chapter is essential. The next section ("Understanding the question") includes smatterings of relatively pedantic analysis, but this is interspersed between more crucial material and thus should be read in its entirety. "The (somewhat) good news" should also be read in full.

Chapter 3: Meaninglessness

The introductory paragraphs of "The bad news" are essential reading, as is the short conclusion. In the bulk of the chapter, sandwiched between these elements, I consider various optimistic responses to the bad news. Impatient readers can pick which of those they wish to read, but I recommend reading them all, with the possible exception of "Nature's 'purposes,'" which may be the least interesting of the optimistic responses.

Chapter 4: Quality

This chapter should be accessible to philosophers and non-philosophers alike. If need be, it may be skipped by those familiar with chapter 3 of either *Better Never to Have Been* or *Debating Procreation*. However, even they should read the first section ("The meaning and quality of life").

Chapter 5: Death

This is by far the longest chapter of the book. Parts of it are also among the most technical (and thus, to some readers, the dullest) parts of the book. Those who do not need convincing that their deaths can be bad for them and who are not interested in the philosophical debates around these issues can skip the sections titled "Is death bad?" and "How bad are different deaths?" that constitute the bulk of the chapter. However, they should know that in skipping those sections, they will miss the arguments that aim at explaining *why* death is bad. I argue that death is bad for more than one reason. One reason is that death deprives one of the good that one would have had if one had not died when one did. The other reason is that death annihilates one—irreversibly ending one's existence. It follows from this that even when death is not bad, all things considered, because it deprives one of insufficient good to outweigh the bad one will suffer, it is nonetheless still bad in one way. It still annihilates one.

Chapter 6: Immortality

This short chapter should be readily accessible to all readers.

Chapter 7: Suicide

Other than the introductory and concluding sections, both of which should be read, this chapter has two broad parts. The earlier one responds to arguments that suicide is never permissible or rational, while the later one broadens the case for suicide as a response to aspects of the human predicament. Those who do not need persuading that suicide is sometimes both permissible and rational could skip the earlier part if necessary. They may nonetheless be interested in reading the later part of the chapter.

Chapter 8: Conclusion

The brief concluding chapter should be read in full.

1 | Introduction

Humankind cannot bear very much reality.

—T.S. ELIOT
"Burnt Norton," Four Quartets

Life's big questions

This book is concerned with life's "big questions"—indeed, the biggest ones: Do our lives have meaning? Is life worth living? How should we respond to the fact that we are going to die? Would it be better if we could live forever? May we, or should we, end our lives earlier—by suicide—than they would otherwise end?

It is difficult to imagine a thinking person who does not, at least one time or another, ponder questions of this kind. Responses to them vary, not only in detail but also in broad orientation. Some people provide ready and comforting answers, whether religious or secular; others find the questions to be insuperably perplexing; while yet others believe that the correct answers to the big questions are generally grim ones.

Although it is inadvisable to scare off one's readers at the beginning of a book, I should disclose at the outset that my views fall mainly into the third category, which is almost certainly the least popular. I shall argue that the (right) answers to life's big questions reveal that the human condition is a tragic predicament— one from which there is no escape. In a sentence: Life is bad, but so is death. Of course, life is not bad in *every* way. Neither is death bad in every way. However, both life and death are, in crucial respects, awful. Together, they constitute an existential vise—the wretched grip that enforces our predicament.

The details of the predicament will be presented in the six chapters that are in between this introduction and the conclusion. However, the broad contours can be summarized here.

First, life has no meaning from a cosmic perspective. Our lives may have meaning to one another (chapter 2), but they have no broader point or purpose (chapter 3). We are insignificant specks in a vast universe that is utterly indifferent to us. The limited meaning that our lives can have is ephemeral rather than enduring.

This is disturbing in itself, but it is even worse because, as I shall argue in chapter 4, our quality of life is as poor as it is. Some lives are obviously worse than others, but even the best lives, contrary to popular opinion, ultimately contain more bad than good. There are compelling explanations why this unfortunate feature of our condition is not widely recognized.

In response to life's cosmic meaninglessness and its poor quality, some might be tempted to think that we must reject another popular opinion, namely that death is bad. If life is bad, then death, it might be argued, must be good—a welcome release from the horrors of life. However, as I argue in chapter 5, we should accept the dominant view that death is bad. The most famous challenges to this view are the Epicurean arguments that death is not bad for the person who dies. The Epicureans did not claim that death is good, but in rejecting their arguments and in endorsing the view that death is bad, I am led to the conclusion that rather than being a (cost-free) solution to the woes of life, death is the second jaw of our existential vise. Death does nothing to counter our cosmic meaninglessness and usually (though not always) detracts from the more limited meaning that is attainable. Moreover, while death does release us from suffering and, for that reason, is sometimes the least bad outcome, it is, even then, a serious bad. This is because the cost of the release is one's annihilation.

Given how bad death is, it should not be surprising that some have sought to cope by denying our mortality. Some think we will be resurrected, or that we will survive death in some new form. Others think that while we are currently mortal, immortality is within scientific reach. In chapter 6, I respond to such delusions and fantasies, and ask whether immortality, if it were attainable, would be good. This question is not settled by the conclusions of chapter 5 because it is possible to think that death is bad but that immortality would also be bad. For example, death could be bad, but immortality might be even worse. I argue that though immortality would indeed be bad under many circumstances, one could imagine conditions under which the *option* of immortality would be good. The fact that we lack the option of immortality under *those* conditions is part of the human predicament.

The discussion of deathly matters continues in chapter 7, but this time, the topic is death by one's own hand. Given that death is bad, suicide is not a solution to the human predicament. However, because death is sometimes less bad than continued life, suicide has its place among possible responses to our predicament. For this reason, we should reject the widespread idea that suicide is (almost) always irrational. Nor is suicide morally wrong as often as it is commonly thought to be. However, even when it is both rational and morally permissible, it is tragic, not only because of its effect on others, but also because it involves the annihilation of the person whose life ends.

Suicide is not the only response to the human predicament. In the final chapter—the conclusion—I consider other responses after defending my extensive (but not unmitigated) pessimistic view about the human condition against some residual optimistic challenges.

Pessimism and optimism

Although my answers to life's big questions are largely pessimistic, it should be noted immediately that the concepts of "optimism" and "pessimism" are vague and thus slippery.

To gain some clarity, one helpful distinction is between different domains within which optimists and pessimists might disagree. One such domain is the realm of the facts. An optimist might believe that some terrible fate will not befall him, whereas a pessimist might believe that he will fall victim to that fate. They both agree that the fate is terrible, but they have differing views about whether it will occur.[1] This particular example is future-oriented. It is about what *will* occur, but disagreements between optimists and pessimists can also be about past or present facts. For example, one can think that more or fewer people were killed in some historic disaster than were actually killed, or one can believe that there are currently more or fewer starving people than there actually are.

Another domain within which optimists and pessimists might disagree is the realm of evaluation of the facts. It is possible for optimists and pessimists to agree on the facts and yet disagree in their evaluations of these facts. The paradigmatic example, hackneyed though it is, is whether the glass is half full or half empty.[2] This is not a disagreement about how much beverage there is in the glass. It is a disagreement about how good or bad those facts are. The optimist declares the state of affairs good because of how much liquid remains, whereas the pessimist mourns the state of affairs because of how much more liquid there could be. If that seems like a trivial case, then consider the following humorous but momentous example: "The optimist proclaims that we live in the best of all possible worlds; and the pessimist fears this is true."[3]

At least with reference to some of the big questions, it is not always clear which of the competing views count as optimistic and which count as pessimistic. This is because the same view can sometimes be spun as either optimism or as pessimism. For example, in chapter 6, I discuss and evaluate the view that an immortal life would be bad because such a life would become tedious. Is such a view pessimistic because it offers a negative evaluation of immortality, or does it count as optimistic because it says that the actual state of affairs—human mortality—is better?

At least some writers have suggested that it is a pessimistic view.[4] I find this usage odd and thus propose to use the terms "optimism" and "pessimism" as follows. Any view of the facts or any evaluation thereof that depicts some element of the human condition in positive terms I shall call an optimistic view. By contrast, I shall describe as pessimistic any view that depicts some element of the human condition in negative terms. (Thus, the claim that immortality would be bad counts as optimistic because it suggests that the fact of mortality is not as bad as we would otherwise think. If we were in fact immortal, then the view that immortality is bad would be pessimistic.)

This usage has a few implications. First, one can be optimistic about one feature of the human condition and pessimistic about another. In other words, the choices are not restricted to being optimistic about every feature or pessimistic about every feature of the human condition. This does not preclude describing an overall view of the human condition as being either optimistic or pessimistic. Such a description would be based on an aggregation of assessments of individual features.[5] When I describe my own position as pessimistic, this is what I mean. It is not to say that I have a pessimistic view about every last feature of human life.

Second, optimism and pessimism are both matters of degree rather than binary positions. If some feature of the human condition is negative, it can be more or less negative. If some other feature is positive, then, similarly, it can be more or less positive.

It should be clear from this that one can be either too optimistic or too pessimistic about the human condition. One is too optimistic if one thinks that things are (or were, or will be) better than they actually are (or were, or will be). One is too pessimistic if one has a more negative assessment than one should have. I shall be arguing that a generally pessimistic view is the more realistic view—that is, the more accurate view.

It should come as no surprise that pessimistic responses to life's big existential questions are unpopular. They are unpopular because they are hard to accept. People do not like to get bad news, at least not about themselves or those emotionally close to them. Indeed, denial is a widespread and well-known response to receiving bad news. But humans have an assortment of other coping mechanisms too. For example, they "look on the bright side of life," as Brian (ironically) admonishes us to do in the final scene of Monty Python's *The Life of Brian* as he is being crucified.

People also rationalize, distract themselves, and create uplifting (religious and secular) narratives that either attempt to explain harsh realities or offer hope of a brighter future, if not in this world then in the next. (This world to come, as I show in subsequent chapters, need not be a religious conception. There are entirely secular conceptions of future idyllic states.)

Yet the overwhelming urge to repeat the optimistic messages, especially in the bleakest times, suggests that they are not quite reassuring enough. It is as if the repetition of the "good news" is essential because it is so at odds with the way the world seems to be. While the optimists have answers to life's big questions, they are not the right ones, or so I shall argue. Their answers are believed, when they are believed, because people so desperately want to believe them, and not because the force of arguments supporting them makes it the case that we must believe them.

Those who do not believe them but who cannot accept the harsh realities remain in a state of bewilderment. They balk at the idea that things could be as bad as the pessimist suggests, but they are also not persuaded by the optimistic spin-doctors.

Life's big questions are big in the sense that they are momentous. However, contrary to appearances, they are not big in the sense of being unanswerable. It is only that the answers are generally unpalatable. There is no great mystery, but there *is* plenty of horror. It is for this reason that I think that the "human *condition*" is most accurately described as the "human *predicament*." Nor is it the case that those who are thrust into this predicament can avoid the horror of it. Limited melioration is sometimes possible, but this is the existential equivalent of palliative care. It addresses some symptoms but not the underlying problem and not without costs.[6]

The human predicament and the animal predicament

The human predicament is not entirely unlike the (sentient) animal predicament more generally. These other animals also suffer and they also die. There are questions to be asked about the meaning of their lives, even though most humans (including those concerned with the meaning of human life and even those concerned about animal suffering) rarely worry whether animal lives have meaning.[7]

Thus, in focusing on the human predicament, I do not mean to suggest that we alone find ourselves in a ghastly situation. Many features of our predicament are shared by the other animals with whom we share an evolutionary history. Indeed, there are many species of animals whose predicament is in many ways much worse than humanity's.

Consider the lives of chickens. The vast majority of male chicks are killed within a day or two after hatching because they are useless to the egg industry. Other chickens live a little longer, but this only protracts their suffering. Broiler chickens are fattened quickly and reach slaughter age within about two months. The lifespan of egg-laying hens is measured in years—typically two—rather than months, but the conditions in which the vast majority live are horrific. Their lives are nasty, brutish, and short, but certainly not solitary. Instead, they are packed together in extremely crowded conditions, causing psychological distress and physical problems.

That the predicament of many (nonhuman) animals is worse than that of many humans does not mean that there are not special features of the human predicament. Although some other animals have a measure of self-awareness, as far as we know, humans have an unparalleled level of it. This means that (cognitively normal adult) humans are able to reflect on their predicament to a degree that other animals are not. They can question the meaning of their own lives, and they can contemplate suicide. Thus, one good reason for focusing on the human predicament is that it has distinctive features that are worthy of examination.

There is also a pragmatic reason for this focus. If one wants people to consider a predicament, one must choose a predicament about which they care. If the consumption of meat and other products from animals, especially those reared in cruel conditions, is a basis for judgment, then most humans do not care much about animals or their predicaments.[8] For example, whether or not animal lives are meaning-deficient is a matter of indifference to most people; this is not the case for the question whether human lives are meaning-deficient. A defense of a pessimistic view about the (nonhuman) animal predicament, sadly, would be of no concern to most humans. By contrast, offering a pessimistic view about the human predicament is a challenge to what most humans care about and is thus more likely to gain their attention.

To tell or not to tell?

There is an obvious dilemma in defending a pessimistic view. If the human predicament is as bad as I shall argue it is, is it not cruel to rub people's noses in it by highlighting just how bad it is? If people have coping mechanisms, should we not indulge them rather than pull the carpet out from under them by telling them just how terrible things are? But should one allow delusions to stand unchallenged? Does a pursuit of the truth not require that one speak honestly rather than engage in polite collusion with what one takes to be untruth?

On one hand, I certainly have no desire to make life worse for people. On the other hand, there is good reason to think that delusions are not innocuous. While they do indeed help people cope, they are also often dangerous. For one thing, they facilitate a reproduction of the human predicament by creating new generations that are thereby thrust into the predicament. In addition, many of the coping mechanisms are often (but not always) bound up with intolerant religious views that cause a great deal of gratuitous suffering—to blasphemers, homosexuals, nonbelievers, and even religious minorities, for example, who may be demonized and subjected to harsh treatment.

This is not to say that all religious people are intolerant and dangerous. Contrary to the views of some aggressive atheists, I do not think that religious views are inherently more dangerous than secular ones. There are many examples of religious people who are tolerant, kind, and compassionate. There are also many examples of committed atheists causing vast amounts of suffering and death, often in pursuit of some secular utopia. These include Mao Zedong, Joseph Stalin, Pol Pot, the Kim dynasty in North Korea, and other devout adherents of atheistic ideologies.

The harm done by optimists, whether religious or secular, is not always this extreme. It need not amount to torturing and killing those who do not accept some or other redemptive ideology. Sometimes, it merely amounts to lesser forms of discrimination and callous responses to the reasonable sensitivities of pessimists. Indulging people's delusions is thus not without cost.

There is therefore a fine line to tread. I do not begrudge private delusions that enable people to cope—as long as these do not harm others. Even when they do harm others, attempts at delusion-busting may be both beyond the bounds of decency and also counterproductive. One does not enter into people's houses of worship to tell them that they are wrong, or knock on people's doors offering to share the "bad news" with them. One does not stop pregnant women on the street and excoriate them and their partners for creating new life.[9] One does not tell young children that they are going to die and that mommy and daddy should not have brought them into existence.

However, writing a book is within the bounds of the acceptable. One contributes arguments to the marketplace of ideas, even though it is a marketplace that is hostile to pessimism, and so the pessimist is at a disadvantage. People's coping mechanisms are so strong that the pessimist has a difficult time getting a fair hearing. Bookshops have entire sections devoted to "self-help" volumes, not to mention "spirituality and religion" and other feel-good literature. There are no "self-helplessness" or "pessimism" sections in bookstores because there is a vanishingly small market for such ideas.

I am not seriously advocating self-helplessness. I think that there are *some* matters about which we are helpless, but even on a realistic pessimistic view, there are things we can do to meliorate (or aggravate) our predicament. Thus, when I refer, tongue in cheek, to self-helplessness books, I really mean an antidote to the psychological snake oil that is peddled, bought, and consumed in large quantities.

A pessimistic book is most likely to bring some solace to those who already have those views but who feel alone or pathological as a result. They may gain some comfort from recognizing that there are others who share their views and that these views are supported by good arguments.[10]

This is not to say that the scales will fall from nobody's eyes. One hopes that at least some readers will come to see the force of arguments for a position that they did not previously hold. Recognizing the human predicament will never be easy. However, as I show in the concluding chapter, there are ways of coping with reality that do not involve denying it.

2 | Meaning

Life has to be given a meaning because of the obvious fact
that it has no meaning.

—HENRY MILLER
*The Wisdom of the Heart (London: Editions
Poetry London, 1947), 11*

Introduction

It is not uncommon for people to fear that their lives are
meaningless—or, at least, to wonder whether they are. Perhaps
such thoughts are rare and fleeting in some people. For others,
they are more common and enduring. Some people are gripped
by existential anxiety or even despair.

However intense and whatever the duration, the concern is
about one's insignificance or the pointlessness of one's life. This
thought often arises from a sense of one's extreme limitedness in
both time and space. We are ephemeral beings on a tiny planet
in one of hundreds of billions of galaxies in the universe (or perhaps the multiverse)—a cosmos that is coldly indifferent to the
insignificant specks that we are.[1] It is indifferent to our fortunes
and misfortunes, to injustice, to our hopes, fears, values, and concerns. The forces of nature and the cosmos are blind.

One's very existence is an extreme contingency. The chances
that a particular human—oneself—would come into existence are

remote. One's ever having come into existence was dependent on a string of contingencies, including the existence of all one's progenitors. Even if all of them, down to one's great-grandparents, grandparents, and parents existed, the odds were still against one's existing. One would not have existed if one's parents had never met, or if they had met but never reproduced, or if they had reproduced but not precisely when they did. In the last case, a different sperm would have united with the ovum of the month to produce some other person.[2]

As unlikely as coming into existence is, nothing could be more certain than ceasing to exist. We can sometimes stave death off for a while, but there is no avoiding it entirely. Every (multicellular) organism that *comes to be* also *ceases to be*. We are doomed from the start.

Moreover, it is thought that there is something absurd about the earnestness of our pursuits. We take ourselves very seriously, but when we step back, we wonder what it is all about. The step back need not be all the way to the cosmos. One does not need much distance to see that there seems something futile about our endless strivings, which are not altogether different from a hamster on its wheel. Much of our lives are filled with recurring mundane activities, the purpose of which is to keep the whole cycle going: working, shopping, cooking, feeding, abluting, sleeping, laundering, dishwashing, bill-paying, and various engagements with ever-expanding bureaucracies.

Even if these mundane activities are thought to serve other goals, the attainment of those goals only yields further goals to be pursued. There is plenty of scope for questioning the significance of even the broader goals of one's life. This (personal) cycle continues until one dies, but the treadmill is intergenerational because people tend to reproduce, thereby creating new mill-treaders. This has continued for generations and will continue until humanity eventually goes the way of all species—extinction. It seems like a long, repetitive journey to nowhere.

In this regard, we seem to be like Sisyphus who, in Greek mythology, was condemned by the gods to pointlessness. His punishment was an endless cycle of rolling a rock to the top of a hill, watching it roll back down, and then having to roll it once again to the top. Many will argue that Sisyphus had it worse because his futile work was so monotonous and because it was for eternity, whereas ours is at least somewhat varied and ends with (individual and collective) extinction. Nevertheless, the apparent absence of any point to our lives suggests to some that our strivings are Sisyphean.

Thoughts of these kinds can be triggered in many ways. The prospect of one's own death, perhaps highlighted by a diagnosis of a dangerous or terminal condition, tends to focus the mind. But the deaths of others—relatives, friends, acquaintances, and sometimes even strangers—can also get a person thinking. Those deaths need not be recent. For example, one might be wandering around an old graveyard. On the tombstones are inscribed some details about the deceased—the dates they were born and died,[3] and perhaps references to spouses, siblings, or children and grandchildren who mourned their loss. Those mourners are themselves now long dead. One thinks about the lives of those families—the beliefs and values, loves and losses, hopes and fears, strivings and failures—and one is struck that nothing of that remains.[4] All has come to naught.

One's thoughts then turn to the present and one recognizes that in time, all those currently living—including oneself—will have gone the way of those now interred. Someday, somebody might stand at one's grave and wonder about the person represented by the name on the tombstone, and might reflect on the fact that everything that person—you or I—once cared about has come to nothing. It is far more likely, however, that nobody will spare one even *that* brief thought after all those who knew one have also died.

It is hard *not* to wonder what it is all about. Yet there are some who believe that all this pessimism is not warranted. My own view is that a deep pessimism about the meaning of life is entirely appropriate, but that this should not be confused with total nihilism about meaning in life. More specifically, we should, as I argue in chapter 3, be nihilistic about an important kind of meaning in life, but, as I argue in the rest of this chapter, there are other kinds of meaning that are attainable with varying frequency and to varying degrees.

Understanding the question

Many people think that questions about the meaning of life are among the most difficult philosophical questions that there are. The meaning of life is often taken to be the ultimate imponderable. *This* particular pessimism is both unfortunate and misguided. Questions such as "Does life have meaning?" or "Can life have meaning?" are notoriously unclear. Indeed, much of the mischief done in responding to such questions results from a failure to gain the requisite clarity. Once we know what we are asking, the broad contours of the answers are reasonably straightforward, at least if we are prepared to be honest with ourselves.[5] That honesty is rare because it requires facing up to some unpleasant truths.

Some people have suggested that the questions about whether life does or can have meaning cannot be made clear because they are themselves meaningless. That is to say, they involve a so-called category mistake.[6] According to this view, life is not something that can have meaning. Words and signs can have meanings, but what they signify cannot. Thus, the word "life" can have a meaning, but what is signified by the word "life" cannot have meaning. Just as it makes no sense to ask about the meanings of lampshades—the objects, not the word—it makes no sense to ask about the meaning of life.

If we were to accept this view, then we would be blocked from asking the question that some (including I) believe has an unpleasant answer. However, the view that questions about the meaning of life involve a category mistake is itself mistaken. The problem is not so much that it takes the question too literally, but that it has too narrow an understanding of the question's possible literal meanings. Among the literal meanings of the word "meaning" are "significance," "importance," and "purpose."[7] When people wonder whether life has (or can have) meaning, they are asking whether our lives are significant, whether they have import, or whether they serve some purpose. Such questions are entirely reasonable and do not involve any confusion.

Although it is coherent to ask questions about the meaning of life, it should already be apparent that these questions can be interpreted in more than one way. Although closely related, "significance," "import," and "purpose" do not have exactly the same meanings. Not all purposes, for example, are (equally) significant or important. Thus, it might make a difference whether one is asking whether life has significance or whether it has importance or whether it has some purpose. And if one were interested in whether life had a purpose, it might matter whether one meant purpose in the sense of "the purpose for which one was brought into existence" or whether one meant purpose in the sense of "the purpose one's life serves (irrespective of whether that is the purpose for which one was brought into existence)."

In general, I shall not be concerned with these specific distinctions as they are less crucial than others. This is because insofar as lives that serve a purpose or are significant or important are not the same thing, the question is really whether lives can have such a conglomeration of features, or at least a number of them.

Thus, I do not plan to specify necessary and sufficient conditions for life to qualify as meaningful. Although that is a task that consumes many analytic philosophers writing on this topic, the effort seems misdirected. This is because we have a very good sense of what the ordinary worry about meaning in life is—and it is not about precisely specified, exceptionless conditions for counting a life as meaningful. Instead, the question is whether there is some significant point to our lives or whether our lives are rather all either pointless or insignificant. Put another way, meaning, as a number of authors have suggested, is about "transcending limits." A meaningful life is one that transcends one's own limits and significantly impacts others or serves purposes beyond oneself.

One way in which a life can have a "point" or be "significant" or "transcend limits" is by making an important mark. However, people can make marks in numerous ways, and many of those marks are moral stains. Indeed, among those who have made the biggest impacts in human history are vast numbers of vile people. Their mark is often death and destruction, as is the case with Adolf Hitler, Joseph Stalin, and Pol Pot, for example. It is the brutal conquerors, tyrants, mass murderers, rapists, and pillagers who exert influence, create empires, and dominate societies. Some of them also leave disproportionate numbers of descendants, another way of transcending their own mortal limits and making a mark on the future. The genes of Genghis Khan, for example, are to be found in about 8% of men living today in those parts of Asia (from the Pacific Ocean to the Caspian Sea) that once constituted his vast empire.[8]

The fact that wicked people make such an impact on human history is bound to cause unease among those who take meaning to be a positive feature of a life. One response is to acknowledge that wicked lives *can* be meaningful, but then say that we should seek only positive meaning. Another option is to say that a life is not meaningful unless its purposes or ways of transcending limits are *positive, worthy,* or *valuable.*[9]

It is sometimes thought that if a life is meaningless, then it also has no value. This is a mistake, although it is easy to see how it arises. If a meaningful life is a life in which limits are transcended in a valuable way, then a life that does not transcend limits in a valuable way might be thought to be without value. However, merely because a life does not transcend limits in a valuable way does not mean that it is not valuable in its own right or valuable to the person whose life it is. Put another way, one does not have to transcend limits in order for one's life to have intrinsic value. Because meaningless lives can have such value, it can be wrong to kill somebody who has failed to make a mark or to have some (important) purpose, for example.

There is sometimes also thought to be a connection between meaning and the quality of life. Whether or not this thought is correct depends, in part, on what one means by quality of life. Meaningfulness does seem to be part of a good life[10] if that is what one means by quality of life. A life with meaning is, all other things being equal, better than one that is meaningless. However, a meaningless life may be sufficiently good in other ways such that its quality is nonetheless not unusually bad. Moreover, if by quality of life, one means its felt quality, then it is entirely possible for a life that objectively lacks meaning to have a good subjective quality, either because the subject does not care about meaning or mistakenly thinks that his[11] life is meaningful. By contrast, when people perceive their lives to be meaningless, there are typically quite profound negative effects on the quality of life.

Questions about meaning in life are understood by some, but not others, as questions about whether life is *absurd*. What divides these opinions, it seems, is not a substantive disagreement, but rather different understandings of the relevant terms. It is possible to stipulate a meaning of "absurd" such that meaningless lives are absurd ones, and it is equally possible to stipulate a different meaning such that lives can be meaningless but not absurd, or absurd but not meaningless.

For example, the philosopher Thomas Nagel thinks that the only lives that can be absurd are those of beings who are capable of viewing their lives not only from the inside but also from an external perspective. What produces the absurdity, he says, is "the collision between the seriousness with which we take our lives and the perpetual possibility of regarding everything about which we are serious as arbitrary, or open to doubt."[12] A mouse's life, he says, cannot be absurd because it is incapable of adopting an external perspective of its life.[13]

This view of absurdity precludes a distinction between (a) one's life being absurd, and (b) one recognizing that one's life is absurd. The former is reduced to the latter. This seems mistaken, not least because it is in conflict with quite common and reasonable views about absurdity, according to which those who are unselfconscious can certainly be absurd. Consider, for example, mindless bureaucrats earnestly turning the cogs of some pointless bureaucracy. We may find the spectacle especially absurd precisely because they have utterly no idea how pointless their activities are. For this sort of reason, I shall allow the possibility that a life can be absurd or meaningless—I shall use the terms interchangeably—without the being whose life it is realizing that it is so.

The most important clarification we require in asking whether life has (or can have) meaning concerns the kind of meaning we have in mind. There are different kinds of meaning, corresponding to different perspectives from which one can ask whether life has meaning (see figure 2.1.).

Thus, we might ask whether life has meaning from the most expansive of perspectives—what is sometimes called the "perspective of the universe," or meaning *sub specie aeternitatis*. Alternatively, we might ask whether life has meaning from a much more limited, terrestrial[14] perspective. There is, in fact, a range of these more limited perspectives. All are radically more limited than the cosmic perspective, but some are more limited than others. It is worth noting some key and representative points on the spectrum.

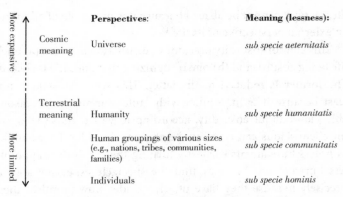

FIGURE 2.1 Perspectives from which life can be judged to have or lack meaning.

The least limited of these perspectives is a human-wide perspective.[15] What is meaningful from this perspective has meaning *sub specie humanitatis.* The perspective of *humanity,* however, is not the only *human* perspective. This is because humanity consists of very many smaller groups, such as nations, tribes, communities, and families. Nations are typically bigger than tribes; tribes are bigger than communities; and communities are bigger than families. Not all groups are geographically localized. Some human groups are international—such as global associations of philatelists or philosophers. For the sake of simplicity, we might lump all these kinds of groups together and view them all as communities of varying sizes and distributions, and thus term lives that are meaningful from some such perspective as having meaning *sub specie communitatis.*[16] The most limited of the human perspectives is the perspective of an individual human.[17] I shall call meaning from this perspective: meaning *sub specie hominis.*[18]

Particular lives can have meaning from some of these perspectives but lack meaning from other perspectives. Failing to recognize and distinguish the different kinds of meaning can thus lead one to think that the absence or presence of one kind of meaning indicates the absence or presence of other kinds of meaning. Before discussing these different perspectives from which we can ask whether life has meaning, some preliminary comments are required.

First, we must avoid taking the term "perspective" too literally. For example, the universe does not literally have a perspective.[19] Nor does humanity as a whole have a perspective in the way in which you or I might have one. Indeed, not every individual necessarily has a perspective. A baby or somebody with advanced dementia may not literally have a perspective, at least under certain interpretations of "perspective." Thus, when we speak about the perspectives of the universe, humanity, communities, or individuals, we are speaking in a metaphorical sense. The real question is whether life has some purpose, impact, or significance at the relevant level.

Second, meaning can be a matter of degree. Thus, life that has some meaning (from a particular perspective) can have more or less of it (from that perspective). In other words, while the usual contrast to "meaningless" is "meaningful," the latter term should not be understood too literally as *full* of meaning. Instead, it should be understood, as it usually is, as having *some* meaning, with varying amounts of meaning being possible.

Third, when we ask whether life has (or can have) meaning, the scope of "life" may vary. We might ask the question about an individual's life, or we might ask it about human life in general, or we might ask it about *all* life (or perhaps only all sentient life). These questions do not all have equal traction (or even application) at all levels. For example, questions about the meaning of all human life (or all life) tend to arise most acutely when asked from the cosmic perspective. People often have anxiety about whether human life in general and their particular individual human lives have any meaning from this perspective. It is much less common for people to worry whether all human life has meaning from the perspective of a given individual or community.[20]

There is another way in which it can make a difference whether one is asking whether an individual life or all (human) life has meaning. Sometimes, the answers stand or fall together. For example, it is probably the case that either no human life has meaning from the perspective of the universe or that all human life does. It is difficult (but not impossible) to see how some but not other human lives would have meaning from this perspective. Put another way, it is difficult to think that one life could have a cosmic purpose but another does not. However, when the question is asked about meaning from the other perspectives, the answer may vary from individual to individual. From the more limited perspectives, some people's lives may be meaningless while others have meaning (to some or other degree).

Fourth, it is helpful to distinguish between (a) perceived meaning, which we might call "subjective meaning" and (b) actual meaning, which we might term "objective meaning." Lives are subjectively meaningful if they *feel* meaningful, and they are objectively meaningful if they meet some condition of meaningfulness that the person living the life may or may not recognize. Implicit in this distinction is the idea that objective meaning is the real meaning and that subjective meaning is merely the appearance of meaning. Thus, we might term the acceptance of this distinction as an objectivist account of meaning.

Not everybody recognizes this distinction. Some people think, either explicitly or implicitly, that actual meaning consists only in the feeling that one's life is meaningful. According to such accounts, which I shall call "subjectivist,"[21] actual meaning reduces to perceived meaning. This leads to bizarre results. Richard Taylor imagines a variant on the story of Sisyphus, in which the gods "waxed perversely mercifully by implanting in him a strange and irrational impulse ... to roll stones."[22] If we accept a subjectivist account of meaning, we would have to accept that, under these circumstances, Sisyphus's life would have become meaningful merely because he would then find his life of stone-rolling immensely meaningful. Yet many of us think that although it would be a satisfying life, it would also be a meaningless one. Similarly, it seems odd to think that lives devoted to watching soap operas, counting hairs on people's heads, or— if still-more-outlandish examples are required—collecting used condoms or tampons would be meaningful even if they were felt to be meaningful by the persons who lived them.

Those who accept the distinction between perceived and actual meaning—and thereby advocate what I shall call an "objectivist" account of meaning—can avoid this kind of problem because they recognize that lives can be meaningless even though they are felt to be meaningful. However, they must also recognize that objectively meaningful lives can be mistakenly perceived as meaningless. Perhaps Franz Kafka is an example of such a person. He seems to have thought very little of his work, published minimally during his life, and left instructions for his friend Max Brod to burn all his unpublished work after his death.

Had Dr. Brod not disobeyed that instruction, Franz Kafka would have remained virtually unknown, and much of his work would have been lost forever. Thus, the life that may have seemed meaningless to Dr. Kafka was objectively meaningful. It follows that objectively meaningful lives can be very unsatisfying.

This has led some to a hybrid of the subjectivist and objectivist views. Susan Wolf, for example, has suggested that "meaning arises when subjective attraction meets objective attractiveness."[23] On such an account, if there is no subjective attraction, there is no meaning.

It is not clear, however, that a hybrid view is the correct response to the problem of what I have called unsatisfying meaningful lives. We might instead stick to the distinction between (a) a life feeling meaningful and (b) a life actually being meaningful. If somebody makes a major contribution but is filled with a sense of meaninglessness, we may regret his lack of satisfaction without denying, as hybrid theorists must, that his life is indeed meaningful. We can affirm that the preferred scenario is one in which a life *is* both meaningful and also *feels* as though it is, without implying that the subjective experience of meaningfulness is *necessary* for the life to be meaningful.

In principle, the distinction between subjectivist and objectivist accounts of meaning cuts across the distinctions between the individual, communal, human, and cosmic perspectives from which lives can be judged to have or lack meaning. That is to say, meaning from each of these different perspectives *could* be either subjective or objective. For example, one can feel as though one's life has or lacks meaning from the cosmic perspective and it can actually be the case that one's life has or lacks meaning from that perspective.

Without denying the life-affecting importance of perceptions of meaningfulness, my primary (but not exclusive) interest is in objective meaning.[24] That is to say, I am mainly interested in whether life actually has meaning from each of the four perspectives I have mentioned. Of these four kinds of meaning, which (if any) might we be able to attain and which (if any) are unattainable? I have bad news and I have *somewhat* good news. I shall delay the bad news until chapter 3 and first share the better news in that which remains of the current chapter.

The (somewhat) good news

In general—although there are exceptions that I shall discuss—the more limited the perspective, the more attainable a meaningful life is. Thus, I begin with meaning from the most limited of perspectives.

Meaning sub specie hominis

We can ask whether life has or can have meaning from the perspective of an individual. One way of understanding this question is whether some individual's life has meaning from the perspective of some *other* individual. The question is then, at least in one phrasing of it, whether this person makes a sufficiently positive impact on some other individual in order to make her life meaningful from that other person's perspective. There are probably some hermits and other radically isolated individuals who may fail to make such a mark, but the vast majority of people make an impact on at least some other individual.

A second way to understand the question is whether some individual's life has meaning from the perspective of the individual whose life it is. According to an objectivist interpretation of this question, a life is meaningful if it fulfills some significant purpose or goal set by the person whose life it is. Perhaps meaning of this kind is not quite as widespread as the first sort of meaning *sub specie hominis*. It is nonetheless within the reach of those many people who do attain some of the goals they set themselves—such as achieving some level of fitness, skill, proficiency, knowledge, or understanding.

Thus, on either interpretation, meaning *sub specie hominis* is attainable, at least for many people. This is not to say that meaning is entirely within one's control. It may be that some people simply cannot get their lives to have meaning. That might be because circumstances conspire against them. Perhaps they fail at everything they attempt. Thus, the claim is not that meaning *sub specie hominis* is within the reach of everybody. Instead, it is only that there are many people who can and do attain meaning from this perspective at least for extensive periods.

Meaning sub specie communitatis

A meaningful life from the perspective of a group of humans is also attainable. In the case of the smallest, most intimate of human groups, the family, meaning is very common. Many people have meaningful lives from this perspective. They are loved and cherished by their family, and in turn they play important, meaningful roles in the lives of those family members. They provide love, support, company, and deep personal connections.

Sadly, this is not true of everybody. There are people with no, weak, or even hostile family relationships, and their lives consequently derive no meaning from the perspective of the family. Nevertheless, it is entirely clear that many other people's lives are meaningful to their children, parents, siblings, grandparents, uncles, aunts, cousins, nephews, and nieces. Their lives serve important, valuable purposes in a family.

Although meaning from the perspective of larger human communities is harder to attain, there are nonetheless many people whose lives are meaningful from this perspective. Many seek and gain meaning by making a mark on local communities, as caring doctors or nurses, devoted teachers, inspiring religious leaders, popular radio personalities, or selfless charitable workers, for example.

It is harder to attain meaning from the perspective of much larger human communities, such as national communities. Making a significant mark here is much more of an achievement. Some succeed, but others do not. (Of course, some of those who do not make a more expansive mark do not seek or want such meaning.)

Making a mark is not identical with being recognized. Think, for example, of secret agents or quiet aid workers who can make significant contributions without attaining recognition at the broad levels at which they make a contribution. Similarly, there are those who are recognized much more widely than their contribution would warrant. There is no shortage of shallow celebrities who are famous merely for being famous. They make a mark on the consciousness of many, but it is an utterly worthless mark.

Talk of meaning from the perspective of a community, and *a fortiori* from the perspective of humanity, might be thought to suggest that activities directed at the wellbeing of (nonhuman) animals,[25] for example, cannot contribute to making a life meaningful. However, such a thought would be mistaken. The more superficial reason is that those who work for the wellbeing of animals can make an indirect but valuable mark on human communities and humanity as a whole. A veterinarian, for example, can make a positive contribution to those humans for whose companion animals he or she cares. An animal rights activist might mitigate or reduce a community's or humanity's moral failures with regard to the treatment of animals.

More important, however, there can, in addition, be meaning from the perspective of an individual animal or a group of animals. I have not included these endless permutations in my (simplifying) taxonomy, but what is said about meaning from various human perspectives may also be said, *mutatis mutandis*, about meaning from various animal perspectives.[26]

Meaning sub specie humanitatis

Relatively few people lead lives that are meaningful from the perspective of all humanity. This is because relatively few people make a significant mark or serve an important purpose when judged from this perspective. Most people's contributions are at a more restricted level. Those who do have a global impact include the likes of the Buddha, William Shakespeare, Florence Nightingale, Albert Einstein, Alan Turing, Jonas Salk, and Nelson Mandela. These, at least, are paradigmatically meaningful lives, *sub specie humanitatis*.

There are also many who have made an important positive impact of global significance but without being well noticed, or even noticed at all. Although examples are, by definition, hard to name, they might include those who facilitated the contributions of the aforementioned by parenting, nurturing, or otherwise teaching them. However, they might also include those who made an unrecognized contribution in their own right. Perhaps, like Alan Turing, they helped shorten a war but, unlike him, their contribution has gone unremarked. Perhaps, like Jonas Salk, they made important scientific breakthroughs but, unlike him, their ideas were stolen by others who were then wrongfully recognized. There may be dissatisfaction and regret for many of those to whom due recognition has not been given, but it remains true that they have made an impact *sub specie humanitatis*.

There are many people who strive for meaning *sub specie humanitatis* but fail to achieve it, or at least fail to achieve it to the desired degree. However, there are clearly some who do succeed in making the sort of global mark that gives their lives meaning from this perspective.

Perhaps some will argue that, in thinking of meaning from this perspective, and perhaps also from the more expansive echelons of meaning *sub specie communitatis*, I am putting too much store in "impact," "leaving a mark," "attaining a goal," or "serving some purpose" at these levels.

To have any plausibility, this objection would need to explain what meaning consists in if not something like having an impact, leaving a mark, attaining a goal, or serving a purpose. Moreover, what we say about meaning *sub specie humanitatis* should be consistent with what we say about meaning from, say, the perspective of a family. If your life has meaning from the perspective of your family because of what you mean to them, then for your life to have meaning from the perspective of all humanity, it must be because of what you mean to humanity. What difference do you make to humanity?

Nobody, of course, should think that they are indispensible. Nobody has *that* much meaning *sub specie humanitatis*. However, there are people who have made a massive difference. Alexander Fleming, for example, made a major contribution to humanity by discovering penicillin, the first antibiotic. Perhaps antibiotics would have been discovered without him, but probably not before many—if not millions—more people would have suffered or died from infections. Even if somebody else would have discovered penicillin when he did, the fact remains that *he* discovered it. *He* made the difference. That gives his work and thus his life meaning *sub specie humanitatis*.

In another possible attempt to broaden the reach of meaning *sub specie humanitatis*, it might be suggested that as long as one's life has meaning from some or other human perspective, it has meaning *sub specie humanitatis*. According to this view, if your life has meaning from the perspective of your family or community, then it has value from the perspective of humanity. Perhaps it will be suggested that this is because your family and community are *part* of humanity, and thus any familial or communal meaning is also meaning from the perspective of humanity. However, that attempt is merely to conflate the different perspectives from which we can judge whether a life is meaningful. What you mean to your parents might be worthy of mention in a family history, but that does not imply that it is worthy of mention in a chronicle of human history.[27] This suggests that while your significance to your parents may give your life meaning from a familial perspective, it does not give your life meaning from the perspective of all humanity.

To this it might be retorted that as long as one's life has meaning from some human perspective, it does have *some* meaning *sub specie humanitatis* even if the meaning from the latter perspective is imperceptible, given the far more expansive perspective. That retort is doomed because it fails to understand that the impact of a life can vary in the ways captured in the metaphor of the different perspectives. A life might impact only an individual or it might (also) have an impact of comparable intensity on a whole community or all of humanity. To think that a life that significantly affects only an individual or community thereby also affects humanity as a whole is to fail to distinguish the kind of impact that a Marie Curie has from the impact of a successful mayor in a small town.

This should not cause us to trivialize or minimize meaning from the perspective of a family or a community. These are valuable forms of meaning, but having meaning from these perspectives should not be confused with having meaning from the broader perspective of all humanity, something that is attained by relatively few.

Conclusion

Thus, the somewhat good news is that our lives can be meaningful—from some perspectives. One reason that this is only *somewhat* good news is that even by the more limited standards, there are some people whose lives either are or feel meaningless. Moreover, the prospects for meaning generally diminish as the scope of the perspective broadens. That the prospects tend to diminish in this way does not imply that lives that are meaningless from a more limited perspective are *never* meaningful from a broader perspective. There are those, for example, who have no family left or who have no meaning for their family or community, perhaps because they have been shunned, but who make an impact at a broader level.

Another reason why the news so far has been only somewhat good is that even those whose lives have meaning from more expansive terrestrial perspectives are rarely satisfied with the amount of meaning their lives have. Not only do people typically want more meaning than they can get, but the most meaning that anybody is capable of attaining is inevitably significantly limited. It is to this bad news that I turn in the next chapter.

3 | Meaninglessness

> Out, out, brief candle!
> Life's but a walking shadow, a poor player
> That struts and frets his hour upon the stage
> And then is heard no more: it is a tale
> Told by an idiot, full of sound and fury,
> Signifying nothing.
>
> —WILLIAM SHAKESPEARE
> *Macbeth, Act 5, Scene 5*

The bad news

The most expansive kind of meaning that we could want for life is what we might call "cosmic meaning." This is meaning from the perspective of the universe—or *sub specie aeternitatis*, as this perspective is sometimes known. Now, as I noted in the previous chapter, speaking literally, the universe itself has no perspective. The universe is not an experiencing subject.[1] It has no point of view. However, the suggestion is not that this "perspective of the universe" be taken literally. It should no more be taken literally than the phrase "a God's eye view" need be taken literally. Atheists can speak of a God's eye view without implying the existence of God. They are speaking about the perspective that God would have if he existed. The cosmic perspective is the view of the cosmos even if nobody actually has that view in its entirety.

Many people who are concerned that life is meaningless are (usually) thinking about meaning from a cosmic perspective, as I illustrated at the beginning of chapter 2. They notice how cosmically insignificant we are. Although we collectively can have some effect on our planet, we have no significant impact on the broader universe.[2] Nothing we do on earth has any effect beyond it. The evolution of life, including human life, is a product of blind forces and serves no apparent purpose. We exist now, but we will not exist for long. That is true of us as individuals, but in the grand sweep of planetary time, let alone cosmic time, it is also true of our species and all life.

Earthly life is thus without significance, import, or purpose beyond our planet. It is meaningless from the cosmic perspective. Because this is true of all life, it is true of all sentient life, all human life, and each individual life. Neither our species nor individual members of it matter *sub specie aeternitatis*. Whatever other kinds of meaning our lives might have, the absence of *this* meaning is deeply disturbing to many.

However, human nature tends to abhor a meaning vacuum—*horror vacui*. There are strong psychological impulses that impel most but not all people to cope with this, either by denying the vacuum or by denying its importance.

The theistic gambit

Arguably, the most ancient and also the most pervasive of these coping mechanisms is theism and associated doctrines. Many theists believe that even if our lives *seem* meaningless from the cosmic perspective, they are not in fact so. This, they say, is because we are not an accident of purposeless evolution, but rather the creation of a God who endows our lives with meaning. According to this view, we serve not merely a cosmic purpose, but a divine one.

This is a seductively comforting thought. For that reason alone, we should be suspicious of it, given how easy it is for humans to believe what they would like to believe.

Many people have raised the objection that theism cannot do the meaning-endowing work it is purported to do here. For example, it has been suggested that serving God's purposes does not suffice, as this makes people "puppets in the hands of a superior agent"[3] or mere instruments to the goals of God.[4] A related objection notes that not merely any divine purpose would give us the kind of meaning we seek. If we had been created "to provide a negative lesson to some others ('don't act like them') or to provide food for passing intergalactic travelers who *were* important,"[5] our lives would not have the sort of cosmic meaning we seek.

The theist might well respond that an omnibenevolent God, who is also omniscient and omnipotent, and who loves us, would have only positive, ennobling purposes for us. He would not create us merely to serve as a negative lesson to others or to provide food for intergalactic travelers. Because of this, the theist could say, there is no problem in being a means to any end set for us by such a God; better to be a means to a supreme being's beneficent purpose than neither to be an end of cosmic significance nor to have any (cosmic) purpose at all.[6]

The problem with such a response is that, insofar as it provides any reassurance about life's cosmic meaning, it does so by providing a hand-waving account of what that meaning is. The account is as mysterious as the ways in which the Lord is often said to move. We are told that serving the purposes of a beneficent deity provides (cosmic) meaning to our lives, but to be told that is not to be told what those purposes are. "Serving God's purposes" is a placeholder for details that need to be provided.

When the details are provided, however, the results are unsatisfactory. If, for example, we are told that our purpose is to love God and serve him, we might reasonably ask why a being as great as God is said to be would possibly want or need the love and service of humans at all—let alone so badly that he would create them to serve that purpose. If loving and serving God is our purpose, the act of creating us sounds like that of a supremely narcissistic rather than a supremely beneficent being. This alleged purpose is thus unconvincing.

Alternatively, we might be told that our divinely endowed purpose—the purpose for which God created us—is to help our fellows. However, while such a purpose might be cosmic in the sense of being endowed by the creator of the cosmos, this particular purpose of the cosmic creator would be distinctly local. Moreover, it would not explain why any of our fellows (whether human or animal) were created. If you were created to help your fellow, and your fellow was created to help you, we are still left wondering why either of you (and by extension any being) was created. This purpose smacks of circularity.[7]

Another possible suggestion is that our purpose on earth is to prepare us for the afterlife. That does not explain what the purpose of the afterlife is. If it is eternal bliss, it might be thought not to require any further end. However, if religious doctrine is to be believed, then for a great many people, the afterlife is not a final good but rather a final bad—hardly the sort of meaning people yearn for. Even in the best-case scenario, it is hard to understand why God would create a being in order to prepare it for an afterlife, given that no afterlife would be needed or desired if the being had not been created in the first place. It is much like a parent creating a child for the purpose of that child's having a satisfying retirement. Satisfying retirements are worth aiming at if one already exists, but they hardly provide grounds for creating people who will have such retirements. The sort of meaning that the afterlife provides cannot explain why God would have created us at all.[8]

As all this illustrates, it is not easy to specify a divinely ordained meaning that convincingly and non-circularly explains the cosmic meaning of human life in a way that affirms rather than demeans humanity. However, even if it were possible to say how God *could* endow our lives with desirable cosmic meaning, a fundamental issue would remain: Do our lives in fact have such meaning? That a God could bestow such meaning does not imply that he exists or that God actually gives our lives the cosmic meaning many humans crave.

Debates about the existence of God are interminable, and I cannot hope to settle them here. In my view, though, the persistence of this debate is not surprising for one reason only: the depth of the widespread human need to cope with the harsh realities of the human predicament, including but not limited to the fact that our lives are meaningless in important ways. Upton Sinclair famously remarked that it "is difficult to get a man to understand something when his salary depends upon his not understanding it."[9] It is similarly difficult to get somebody to understand something when the meaning of his life depends on his not understanding it.

Some will ask how I can know that our lives lack cosmic meaning.[10] They may suggest that I should instead say that "perhaps there is ... [such] meaning, but I personally can't imagine what it could be."[11] If we assume, for the moment, that that objection has merit, it would be a noteworthy feature of the human predicament that, even if human life does have cosmic meaning, humans cannot know what it is. Having to live in fear that one's life is cosmically meaningless is an unfortunate condition for beings that yearn for the confidence that their lives are cosmically meaningful.

That would be bad enough. Things are still worse because the objection is misguided. Obviously none of us can be *certain* that life has no cosmic meaning, but to claim to know something is not to claim that one could not possibly be wrong. I cannot be certain that the following claim is untrue: "Seventy-five million years ago, Xenu, a tyrant who ruled a 76-planet galactic federation, had his officers capture and then freeze beings of all shapes and sizes in the confederation; billions of them were then transported to earth (then called Teegeeack) in aircraft, thrown into volcanoes and then had hydrogen bombs dropped on them."[12] Yet there is no evidence to support this claim, and thus I can reasonably say that (I know that) it did not happen, even though I cannot be absolutely certain.

In any event, as the claim about Xenu illustrates, there is no limit to the possible claims religions can make. Even religious people need to sort between all the claims that are made, deciding which to reject and which, if any, to accept. In rejecting some, they are saying (they know or at least believe) that those claims are false.

It would indeed be wonderful if there were a beneficent God who had created us for good reason and who cared for us as a loving parent would for his or her children. However, the way the world is provides us with plenty of evidence that this is not the case.

Imagine you were to visit a country in which the evidence of repression is pervasive: There is no freedom of the press or expression; vast numbers of people live in squalor and suffer severe malnutrition; those attempting to flee the country are imprisoned; torture and executions are rampant; and fear is widespread. Yet your minder tells you that the country, the "Democratic People's Republic of Korea," is led by a "Great Leader" who is an omnibenevolent, infallible, and incorruptible being who rules for the benefit of the people. Other officials endorse this view with great enthusiasm. There are impressive rallies in which masses of people profess their love for the Great Leader and their gratitude for his magnificent beneficence. When you muster the courage to express skepticism, citing various disturbing facts, you are treated to elaborate rationalizations that things are not as they seem. You are told either that your facts are mistaken or that they are reconcilable with everything that is believed about the Great Leader. Perhaps your minder even gives a name to such intellectual exercises—"Kimdicy."[13]

It would be wonderful if North Korea were led by an omnibenevolent, infallible, and incorruptible ruler, but if it had such a leader, North Korea would look very different from the way it does look. The fact that many people in North Korea would disagree with us can be explained by either their vested interests in the regime, by their having been indoctrinated, or by their fear of speaking out. The presence of disagreement between them and us is not really evidence that deciding the matter is complicated.

Not all of earth is as bad as North Korea, but North Korea is part of "God's earth"; so are Afghanistan, Burma, China, Iraq, Saudi Arabia, Somalia, Syria, and Zimbabwe, to name but a few appalling places for many to live.[14] Even in the best parts of the world, terrible things happen. Assaults, rapes, and murders occur, injustices are perpetrated, and children are abused. Fortunately, the incidence of such evil in places like Western Europe is lower than in worse places on earth, but my point is that they all occur within the jurisdiction of a purportedly omnipotent, omniscient, and omnibenevolent God. Nor should we forget the horrific diseases from which people suffer around the globe, or the fact that every day, billions of animals are killed and eaten by other animals, including humans.

The numbers are so staggering that we cannot even compute them. However, to get some sense, consider that one study found that common dolphins and striped dolphins along the Atlantic coast of the Iberian Peninsula consume 27,500 tons of sardines, gadids, hake, and scads annually. That is over 75 tons of fish per day—by only two kinds of predators in one corner of the world's oceans. Globally, sperm whales are (conservatively) estimated to consume 100 million tons of cephalopods.[15] The annual loss of wildebeest to predators is estimated to be 42% of this prey species' total biomass.[16] The overwhelming majority of turtle hatchlings are eaten or otherwise die after surfacing from their sandy nests before they can make the few-minute scamper into the ocean. More die in the mouths of ocean predators. "The little turtles come out into a world anxious to eat them."[17]

These numbers, which are but a few examples, should not cause us to forget the severity of the suffering for individual animals. It varies, of course. Some prey die instantly. For others, death is protracted. Consider the following description:

> The lioness sinks her scimitar talons into the zebra's rump. They rip through the tough hide and anchor deep in the muscle. The startled animal lets out a bellow and its body hits the ground. An instant later the lioness releases her claws from its buttocks and sinks her teeth into the zebra's throat, choking off the sound of terror. Her canine teeth are long and sharp, but an animal as large as a zebra has a massive neck, with a thick layer of muscle beneath the skin, so although the teeth puncture the hide they are too short to reach any major blood vessels. She must therefore kill the zebra by asphyxiation, clamping her powerful jaws around its trachea (windpipe), cutting off the air to its lungs. It is a slow death . . . the zebra's death throes will last five to six minutes.[18]

Some animals are eaten alive. In the following description, the victim is an adult blue whale:

> The beleaguered whale, trailing streams of blood from several wounds, is flanked on either side by three or four individuals. Two more swim ahead and three behind. A squadron of five killer whales takes turns patrolling under the blue whale's belly, preventing it from diving. Three more swim over its head, discouraging it from raising its blowhole above the surface, thereby hampering its breathing. Dominant males lead sorties to rip off slabs of blubber and flesh. They have already shredded its tail flukes.[19]

This continues for over five hours.

This does not look like a world created by a beneficent deity with unbounded knowledge and power. It is credulous to believe that things are not the way they seem and that the world was created by such a being.

The (nonhuman) animal predicament is particularly revealing. Confronted with the awful spectacle of billions of animals being eaten, often alive, by predators, humans typically do not attempt to propose any cosmic meaning to *those* lives. Indeed, the usual monotheistic response is to say that the (or at least one) purpose of animals is to be eaten by others higher up the food chain. It is hard to reconcile that with the existence of a purportedly benevolent God, who surely *could* have created a world in which billions did not have to die each day to keep others alive.[20] And if one thought that a benevolent God did create some animals as food for others, it should at least weaken one's confidence that God would have a satisfying purpose for humans.

The common response here is that humans are special, and thus God would have a special purpose for them. However, postulating such a massive discontinuity in cosmic meaning between humans and nonhuman animals presupposes the very religious commitments that are in question—namely, that humans are the capstone of God's creation, rather than a product of the same evolutionary process that produced every other species.[21]

It is not uncommon for theists to treat life's meaninglessness as a *reductio ad absurdum* of atheism. According to such arguments, denial of God's existence has such horrific implications that such denial must be mistaken.[22] It is not at all clear that atheism has all the implications that are attributed to it,[23] but those advancing the argument fail to take seriously the possibility that any genuine implications of atheism that are unpalatable may indeed be true. It is much more likely, given the evidence, that our lives lack cosmic meaning than that God exists. Theism might provide comfort, but its existential anesthesia comes at a veritable cost.

It is not only theists who seek relief from anxiety about cosmic meaninglessness. There are many secular arguments that are intended to provide or have the effect of providing such relief. By secular arguments, I do not mean only those that actively deny the claims of religion, but more generally those that do not presuppose religious claims.

Nature's "purposes"

For example, it has been suggested that it is a mistake to suppose that, without God, there can be no ultimate purpose. Stephen Law says that every other living organism has a purpose, namely, "to reproduce and pass on its genetic material to the next generation."[24] He says that we "each exist for a purpose, a purpose supplied by nature, whether or not there is a God."[25]

If that were our ultimate purpose, it would not be sufficiently ultimate to count as a cosmic purpose. Instead, it would be a distinctly terrestrial purpose. Nor would this purpose be inspiring enough to console us. When people wonder whether their lives have meaning, they are not likely to be reassured by the observation that they are (merely) a mechanism for replicating genetic material. Indeed, that is the very kind of thought that drives people to wonder what life is all about. To think that humans would find genetic replication a satisfactory cosmic purpose is as absurd as the quip that a chicken is an egg's way of making another egg.

Most important, however, to suggest that our nature-endowed purpose is to pass on genetic material to the next generation is to mischaracterize what a purpose is. A purpose is something endowed by a being capable of having goals. Such beings, which include humans and some animals, and would include a God if one existed, create things to serve the purposes they have for them, or they use preexisting things for some purpose.

For example, the purpose of a paperclip is to hold papers together. Its existence and attributes are explained by the fact that humans created it to function in this way. However, paperclips can also be used for other purposes to which goal-directed beings might put them. Thus, we might unfold a paperclip and use one end of it to depress a reset button on an electronic device. That was not why paperclips were created, but we can endow a paperclip with this alternative purpose by using it to attain our goal of resetting the machine. Furthermore, things never created for any purpose can subsequently be endowed with one. A rock might be used for the purpose of hammering something even if it was never created for that purpose. Nature, however, has no goals. It is a blind process that unfolds without any end in mind. It neither intends our existence nor has any goal at which our existence is aimed.

Nature might help us explain our existence, but that explanation is a causal one rather than a purposive one.[26] It imputes no purposes, at least not in a literal sense, to anybody or anything. It merely provides an explanation of *how* rather than *why* we came to exist.[27] We might find it interesting to know how humans evolved and replicated, but understanding this does not imply that there is a nature-endowed purpose to our existence.

It is true, of course, that many (but by no means all) of us were brought into existence for a creator-endowed purpose. The relevant creators were our parents.[28] They might have created us for any number of purposes—to fulfill their desires for genetic offspring, to have a child to rear, to silence their parents' pleas for grandchildren, to pass on particular values or ways of life, or to contribute to the survival or growth of an ethnic or national group, for example. However, these are the purposes of our parents rather than of nature. Nor are they purposes of cosmic significance.

Scarce value

There is another, more sophisticated attempt to argue that our lives have cosmic meaning—or at least that they *may* have such meaning. The core of the philosopher Guy Kahane's argument takes the following form:

1. We possess value.
2. If there is no other life in the universe, then nothing else has value.
3. If nothing else has value, then we possess the most value.
4. Therefore, if there is no other life in the universe, we have immense cosmic significance.[29]

Dr. Kahane says that although there is disagreement about the basis for our having value, the first premise enjoys widespread support. He notes, however, that it is ambiguous. It—or, more specifically, the word "we"—"can refer to terrestrial sentient life in general, or it can refer only to us humans."[30] If earth is the only place where life is found, then *all* terrestrial sentient life has great cosmic significance. Those who want to say that humans possess greater cosmic significance than their fellow earthlings "must further claim that our intelligence and the achievements and failures it makes possible are associated with a distinctive, superior kind of value."[31]

These and other comments[32] suggest that although Dr. Kahane avoids explicating why we have value, he seems to think that it derives from sentience and possibly also from sapience (that is, wisdom or intelligence).[33] Basing our value on such attributes is necessary to ensure the truth of the second premise by ruling out the view that inanimate objects, natural formations, and systems also have value. If these possessed value, then other parts of the universe would be replete with value. Consider, for example, the Milky Way, Saturn's rings, or Olympus Mons, a mountain on Mars that is the tallest mountain in our solar system, standing nearly two-and-a-half times the height of Mount Everest.

Dr. Kahane is clear that, because we do not know whether we are alone in the universe, we do not know whether we have the massive cosmic significance supported by the conditional conclusion of his argument. If there is abundant life elsewhere, then our significance is considerably reduced. Thus, the argument is intended to show only that our lives *may* have great cosmic significance. Ironically, our lives could have this significance, according to Dr. Kahane's argument, only if God does *not* exist, for if there were a God, our significance in the cosmos would be dwarfed by God's significance.[34]

The conclusion of Dr. Kahane's argument may be (superficially) comforting to those who fear that a godless world is one in which our lives are cosmically meaningless. However, the argument has a number of problems, most importantly ones pertaining to the inference from the premises to the conclusion. The upshot of this is that the conclusion fails to provide the comfort it first seems to offer.

The argument's premises are concerned with value, whereas the conclusion makes a claim about significance. Dr. Kahane realizes that significance is not the same as value,[35] but this does not prevent him from making the unwarranted inference. He correctly notes that although "claims about significance ... are related to claims about value,"[36] something's being valuable is not sufficient for it to have significance. It also "needs to be *important*, to *make a real difference*."[37]

Thus, part of the problem is that it is possible to possess the *most* value without possessing *much* value. Even if we were the most valuable beings in the universe, it would not follow that we are immensely valuable. The value we do have would not be increased by the fact that there was nothing else of value. By analogy, the bowhead whale is the animal species with the *longest* lifespan of all earthlings, perhaps living up to or beyond two centuries. If it also has the longest lifespan in the universe, it would not follow that the lifespan is immense (when judged by the standards of cosmic time).

However—and this is the more important point—even if our lives do have immense value, it does not follow that they have immense cosmic *significance*. Whether they do depends on what one means by cosmic significance. It is not at all clear what Dr. Kahane means by it, and this is because he slips from speaking about value to speaking about significance. However, there are places where he seems to be speaking about our mattering morally—our being morally considerable.[38]

If that is what is meant, then we can say that moral agents, wherever they might be in the cosmos, should desist from actions that would wrongfully harm us, and that they should do so because we have (moral) value. It would not matter if they could not see us, just as it does not matter that we cannot see remote people on earth whom we might wrongfully harm by performing some action. In this sense, our value could be significant in some distant corner of the universe, just as it is significant in some distant corner of our globe. Our value can extend a moral claim to a moral agent anywhere in the cosmos (if there are any such agents elsewhere in the cosmos).

However, that is simply not the sense of "significance" that people have in mind when they are concerned about human cosmic insignificance.[39] Instead, people are concerned that the universe (including our own planet and its powerful natural forces) is indifferent to us, that nothing we do makes any difference beyond our planet or in cosmic time, and that human life has no purpose.[40]

In other words, the existential concerns people have are not the sorts that are dependent on how much other life the universe contains. Knowing that there is no life anywhere else in the cosmos would bring no solace to those who fear that human life is cosmically meaningless.

Nor will such people be comforted by an argument that concludes not only that we have immense cosmic meaning but that toads do too. Even if one thinks that humans may have more cosmic meaning than toads can have, it is still the case, according to the argument, that if humans have immense cosmic meaning, toads also have impressive cosmic meaning.

Dr. Kahane's argument has another odd implication. According to his argument, how much significance human life has depends, at least in part, on how much other life there is. If there is no extraterrestrial life, then human life would have immense cosmic significance. However, we know that earth is teeming with life. It follows, therefore, that human life would have much less terrestrial significance than cosmic significance.[41] (Human life would have less terrestrial significance because there are also aardvarks, elephants, llamas, and zebras, for example.) This is the exact opposite of what we usually think. We usually, and plausibly, think that we have a much greater impact on our planet than we do on the rest of the cosmos, and that although our planet is as indifferent to us as the rest of the universe, we are at least able to exercise more control over our planet than we are over other parts of the universe.

Perhaps Dr. Kahane realizes that the kind of cosmic significance he thinks we might have is not the sort that people seek. After all, he says that he does "not mean to deny that the universe we inhabit is bleak, blind and indifferent."[42]

Discounting the cosmic perspective

Not all arguments aimed at providing secular comfort claim that our lives have cosmic meaning. Some attempt to undermine the relevance of the cosmic perspective. For example, Thomas Nagel responds to a number of thoughts that prompt pessimism about our cosmic significance. First, he argues that if it is true that "nothing we do now will matter in a million years ... then by the same token, nothing that will be the case in a million years matters now."[43]

However, this response seems too glib, at least if it is viewed as a response to the position I am defending. It is not infrequently the case that the significance of what we do now is influenced, if not determined by, whether it will matter later. For example, one might wonder whether to spend the morning writing philosophy or instead waste the time. In an important sense, it really does not matter now which option one chooses. If one indulges oneself, nothing bad will come of it now or tomorrow. But it will matter later. More specifically, it will matter later whether one used one's time wisely or frivolously. Because it matters later, it also (instrumentally) matters now.

Similarly, sometimes things do not matter now because they will not matter later. For example, it might not matter that one has prostate cancer if one is old enough and likely to die from something else before the cancer becomes symptomatic. (It is said that many men die *with* rather than *from* prostate cancer.) It also does not matter if one does not fix the cracks on a building that will soon be demolished, and it does not matter now because it will not matter later.

Or consider somebody who dies in battle. Whether that death was meaningless or not depends, at least in part, on whether it matters later. If that battle has no effect on the war or if the war is eventually lost, then the death of that soldier was meaningless. Perhaps the soldier exhibited bravery and inspired his comrades, but his death was nonetheless ultimately in vain. It did not achieve any long-term purpose.

Thus, we see that an eye on what will matter in the future sheds at least some light on what matters now. It is true, of course, that the foregoing examples of this do not involve adopting the cosmic perspective, but that difference is less important if we accept the most reasonable interpretation of the existential concern.

So understood, the claim is not that *nothing* matters now. Professor Nagel is correct that chains of "justification come repeatedly to an end within life"[44] and that "[n]o further justification is needed to make it reasonable to take aspirin for a headache, attend an exhibition of the work of some painter one admires, or stop a child from putting his hand on a hot stove."[45] Instead, the claim is that while these activities do matter, they *only* matter now—during the lives of those affected. Chains of justification can end within a life making various actions within the life entirely reasonable. However, the bigger existential questions are about whether the life as a whole has any purpose. To answer that question, it is not sufficient to point to justifications internal to the life.

Consider an analogy. If one is playing a game of backgammon, it is entirely reasonable to make various moves. Indeed, one is not playing backgammon unless one is making (permitted) moves. There are justifications for this move and for that one. It is an entirely different matter to ask what the point of backgammon is, whether one should be playing backgammon at all, and whether one should pass it on to the next generation (by teaching it to children—or by creating children to whom one can teach it). Similarly, it can be entirely reasonable to relieve headaches and prevent harms to children and yet worry that one's life as a whole—or human life in general—has no cosmic purpose. The absence of cosmic meaning may provide one with a reason to regret one's existence or to desist from perpetuating the whole pointless trajectory by abstaining from bringing new people into existence.

Professor Nagel also takes issue with other pessimistic arguments about life's cosmic meaning. He argues that our limits in space and time do not matter in the way that many people think they do. Thus, he asks rhetorically: "would not a life that is absurd if it lasts seventy years be infinitely absurd if it lasted through eternity?[46] And if our lives are absurd given our present size, why would they be any less absurd if we filled the universe . . . ?"[47]

Those responses sound superficially plausible, but they fail to engage with what generates the existential questions. The quest for meaning is, as Robert Nozick notes, a quest for transcending "the limits of an individual life."[48] This is true at all levels, not only cosmic meaning. We seek purpose in family, in broader communities, and in contributions to humanity—all ways of transcending one's own limits. Many humans also have the futile desire for purpose at a cosmic level. The quest for meaning would not arise if we were not limited. God, presumably, would not worry about the meaning of his life. God would not worry whether he was fulfilling some external purpose.

Indeed, it is comically absurd to think of God having this sort of existential anxiety, but we can well understand how a limited (self-conscious) being might want to transcend his or her own limits. Imagine that you had no temporal limit—that you were immortal. Under those circumstances, the purposes internal to your life might well suffice. Because you would endure, there would be no need to seek a purpose that survived your personal extinction. Temporal limits seem more problematic than spatial ones, but a comparable point can be made about the latter. If you were spatially unlimited then, of necessity, there would be nothing spatially beyond you, and there would be no need to seek purpose beyond one's own spatial limits. The whole project of transcendence makes sense only if one is limited.

Once we see this, we understand why Professor Nagel's responses are problematic. An absurd life of seventy years would not necessarily be infinitely absurd if it lasted an eternity. It really depends on the kind of absurdity one has in mind. (I assume here, as before, that an absurd life is a meaningless one.) Some lives are absurd even from various terrestrial perspectives. If they were of infinite duration, they would indeed be infinitely absurd. Thus, immortality by itself is not sufficient to make a life cosmically significant. However, there are lives that are not absurd from more limited perspectives, but are absurd from a cosmic perspective, and they are absurd from that broader perspective in part because there is a temporal limit that they cannot transcend. Those lives would *not* be infinitely absurd if they lasted an eternity, at least if the meaning could be sustained or evolve over eternity. Instead of the meaning of a life ending, it would continue in some form in perpetuity. Such lives would, at least in this respect, cease to be absurd (that is, meaningless) from the cosmic perspective.

Imagine somebody trying to burrow through (or under) the reinforced concrete walls of a prison. His ardent labor is absurd only if he fails to breach the wall and escape. If he does transcend the limits imposed by the wall, the labor ceases to be absurd. By the same token, transcending one's temporal limits would be to overcome one feature of one's existence that renders one's labors absurd (from the cosmic perspective).

Professor Nagel's point about our size is similarly unfair. When people ponder their insignificant size in the vast cosmos, the point is not so much size as limit. If the universe consisted of you and you alone, you would not be limited in this way (unless there was something beyond the universe), and it would be incoherent to want to transcend a limit you did not have. This point is satirized if it is reduced to comparing your current size relative to the universe and your filling the universe.

Focusing on terrestrial meaning

Another common and related strategy for downplaying the importance of the cosmic perspective is to frame questions about meaningfulness in life exclusively in terms of terrestrial meaning. Many of those who employ this strategy do not explicitly argue that the cosmic perspective is irrelevant and that we should focus exclusively on terrestrial perspectives. Instead, they frame the entire issue of meaningfulness of life in terms of terrestrial meaning, implicitly assuming that questions concerning the meaning of life are questions only about this kind of meaning.[49] In so doing, they beg the key question. They assume a formulation of the question that, as we have seen, enables an optimistic answer. They ignore a fuller formulation of the question—one that will require an explicit confrontation with the ugly truth that our lives lack the cosmic meaning for which humans so often yearn.

Others who employ the strategy of focusing on terrestrial meaning do not entirely ignore the specter of cosmic meaninglessness. Instead, they attempt to redirect our focus to terrestrial meaning.

Peter Singer, for example, says that meaning is to be found in "working for . . . a 'transcendent cause', that is, a cause that extends beyond the boundaries of the self."[50] We need to transcend those boundaries by doing something that is worth doing.[51] He takes ethical causes to be paradigmatic (but not the only) examples[52] of what is worth doing. All his examples, though, are ones that have meaning from some terrestrial perspective. He recognizes our cosmic insignificance but notes, for example, that "the fact that the most beautiful and enduring of human artefacts will eventually turn into dust is not a reason for denying that its creation was a worthwhile and meaningful task."[53] In other words, it does not matter that our achievements will not last forever.

This discounting of the cosmic perspective is akin to Thomas Nagel's and subject to the same criticism. His discounting of the cosmic perspective would have force against a view that the only meaning is cosmic meaning and thus that anything that lacks cosmic meaning is meaningless tout court. One can respond to such a view, as Peter Singer has, by saying that some tasks are worthwhile and meaningful even if their meaning will not last forever.

However, this response simply does not engage with those who adopt the more nuanced position I have outlined. According to this position, many activities and lives have terrestrial meaning, but our lives still lack meaning *sub specie aeternitatis*. Those who adopt this position can say to optimists like Professor Singer: "Yes, we know that many activities are meaningful *sub specie communitatis* and *sub specie humanitatis*, and we are pleased about that, but we are alarmed that our lives have no cosmic meaning. Nothing you have said allays that concern."

Consider another analogy. If you are worried about your
father's health, it does not make you less worried about his
health if you are told that your mother is entirely healthy. It
is obviously good that your mother is healthy. If she were not,
you would worry about that too. However, being told that you
need not worry about her health does not diminish your worry
about his. Similarly, while things would be much worse if our
lives lacked any meaning, those who are concerned about the
absence of cosmic meaning are not consoled *about that* by the
observation that at least some kinds of terrestrial meaning are
attainable.

The point can be expressed another way. I may derive some
meaning from helping another person, and that person may
derive some meaning from helping a third person, but that provides no point to our collective existence. We can still say that
human life in general is meaningless *sub specie aeternitatis*. There
would be something circular about arguing that the purpose of
humanity's existence is that individual humans should help one
another. Moreover, even if an individual human's life has some
terrestrial meaning (perhaps by helping others), it does not follow that that individual's life also has cosmic significance.

Sour grapes and varieties of meaning worth wanting

I have argued that cosmic meaning is unattainable. The final optimistic response to this is to deny that we should either be seeking cosmic meaning or regretting that we do not have it. I loosely
classify moves of this kind as "sour grapes" arguments (although

those who advance such arguments would of course reject the sour grapes appellation).

The argument comes in varying forms. One form, often only implicit, is that it is not worth worrying about the unattainable, as such worry will not yield any good. The problem with this, however, is that if it is not worth seeking something that one cannot attain, it can still be appropriate to regret the unattainable. Consider a terminal patient for whom there is no cure. Getting better is not attainable, yet that person may very reasonably regret having a terminal condition.

Perhaps, however, regret is reasonable in such a case because it is possible to imagine an alternative situation in which one were not going to die imminently. It is a scenario in which one never acquired the illness that will soon kill one. Such a scenario may be unattainable in practice, but because it is conceivable, there is some possible alternative state of affairs that one regrets is not the actual state of affairs. Regretting the absence of cosmic meaning, it is sometimes argued, is very different from this because there is no conceivable way our lives could have cosmic meaning.

Christopher Belshaw, for example, says that because even "God isn't ultimate enough" to solve our meaning worries, "we should conclude ... that such worries are simply not real."[54] In another deployment of this kind of argument, Guy Kahane asks rhetorically whether "the idea is supposed to be that to be cosmically significant, we need to be moving galaxies around?"[55]

One problem with this sort of argument is that those advancing it may simply not have settled on what would make life meaningful from the most expansive perspective. However, the argument fails even if we assume that there is nothing that could make our lives cosmically meaningful. It fails not because the premise is false but because a comforting conclusion does not follow. If our lives are irredeemably meaningless *sub specie aeternitatis*, and no conceivable alternative circumstances could have made things otherwise, it is still the case that our lives are (cosmically) meaningless. The meaninglessness is then so deep a part of the human predicament that it simply could not have been otherwise. That is terrible news, not good news.

According to a third version of the sour grapes argument, desire for cosmic meaning suggests some defect in the person who has the desire. For example, Susan Wolf speaks (in passing) of "an irrational obsession with permanence"[56] and Guy Kahane suggests that "there is more than a touch of narcissism in this wish for cosmic celebrity"[57] and that the desire for grand cosmic significance is "embarrassingly megalomaniac"[58]—akin to the "madmen pretending to be Napoleon or Jesus.[59]

The most plausible candidates for the "megalomaniac" description are those who believe that we *do* have cosmic significance, not those who believe that we do not. But is the *desire* for such meaning (and the regret that we lack it) narcissistic and megalomaniacal? We do not typically think that those who want but lack familial or communal meaning are narcissistic or megalomaniacal. Thus, it seems that at least part of the explanation why a desire for cosmic meaning is thought to reflect badly on the desirer is precisely that it is unattainable. However, I see no reason why we should not regret the absence of some good merely because it is unattainable. A predicament can be lamented even if it is unavoidable. Just because we cannot have cosmic meaning does not mean that we should not think it would be good to have.

Meaning from the cosmic perspective would be good for extensions of the same reasons that meaning from the other perspectives is good. People, quite reasonably, want to matter. They do not want to be insignificant or pointless. Life is tough. It is full of striving and struggle; there is much suffering and then we die. It is entirely reasonable to want there to be some point to the entire saga. The bits of terrestrial meaning we can attain are important, for without them, our lives would be not only meaningless but also miserable and unbearable. It would be hard to get up each day and do the things that life necessitates in order to continue. One writer has sniffed at this suggestion, saying that the "idea that the natural consequence of finding one's life meaningless is to commit suicide is somewhat ridiculous."[60] In fact, however, failed social belonging is, at least according to some, the most important factor in predicting suicide.[61] Failed social belonging is one consequence of perceiving one's life to have no meaning from the perspective of some other humans.

Viktor Frankl, a psychiatrist who survived various concentration camps, including Auschwitz, highlighted the importance of meaning—or, more accurately, *perceived* meaning.[62] Writing of his experiences during the Holocaust, he argued that meaning was crucial to survival. In his view, there "is nothing in the world . . . that would so effectively help one to survive even the worst conditions as the knowledge that there is meaning in one's life."[63] He says that "Nietzsche's words 'He who has a *why* to live for can bear with almost any *how*' could be the guiding motto for all psychotherapeutic and psychohygienic efforts regarding prisoners."[64] While the conditions of concentration camp inmates were extreme, he affirms the more general point that "the striving to find a meaning in one's life is the primary motivational force in man."[65]

Although we need at least some terrestrial meaning, it is unsurprising that this does not give us everything that it would be good to have. The meaning we have from various human perspectives does not give meaning to the entire human enterprise. It does not provide a point to the entire species and its continued existence. If there is no point to the species and each one of us is but a cog in the machinery of a pointless enterprise, then there is a serious deficit of meaning even if our lives are not without some (terrestrial) meaning. The terrestrial meaning is good, but the absence of cosmic meaning is bad.

Conclusion

There are some who will characterize my view as "nihilistic."[66] Left unqualified, that characterization is false. My view of *cosmic* meaning is indeed nihilistic. I think that there is no cosmic meaning. If I am right about that, then calling me a nihilist about cosmic meaning is entirely appropriate. However, my view is not nihilistic about *all* meaning because I believe that there is meaning from some perspectives.

Our lives can be meaningful, but only from the limited, terrestrial perspectives. There is a crucial perspective—the cosmic one—from which our lives are irredeemably meaningless. In thinking about meaning in life, two broad kinds of mistakes are made. There are those who think that the only relevant meaning is what is attainable. They ignore our cosmic meaninglessness or they find ways either to discount questions about cosmic meaning or to minimize the importance of cosmic meaninglessness. The other kind of mistake is to think that because we are cosmically insignificant, "*nothing* matters," where the implication is that nothing matters from any perspective. If we lack cosmic meaning but have other kinds of meaning, then some things *do* matter, even though they only matter from some perspectives. It does make a difference, for example, whether or not one is adding to the vast amounts of harm on earth, even though that makes no difference to the rest of the cosmos.

Life is meaningless, but it also has meaning—or, more accurately, meanings. There is no such thing as *the* meaning of life. Many different meanings are possible. One can transcend the self and make a positive mark on the lives of others in myriad ways. These include nurturing and teaching the young, caring for the sick, bringing relief to the suffering, improving society, creating great art or literature, and advancing knowledge.

We are nonetheless warranted in regretting our cosmic insignificance and the pointlessness of the entire human endeavor.[67] As impressed as (some) humans often are about the significance of humanity's presence in the cosmos, our absence would have made absolutely no difference to the rest of the universe.[68] We serve no purpose in the cosmos and, although our efforts have some significance here and now, it is seriously limited both spatially and temporally.

Even those who think that we ought not to yearn for the greater meaning that is unattainable must recognize the immense tragedy of beings who suffer such existential anxiety over their insignificance. That suffering is indisputably a part of the human predicament.

4 | Quality

What a distance there is between our beginning and our end! The one, the madness of desire and the seduction of voluptuousness; the other, the destruction of all our organs and the fetid odour of decaying cadavers. Moreover, the road of well-being between the one and the other goes ever downwards: the blessed, dreaming childhood, happy youth, the tribulations of those in their prime, frail and often pathetic old age, the torment of the last illness, and finally the agony of dying. Therefore does it not seem that Being is a misstep . . . ?

—ARTHUR SCHOPENHAUER
Parerga und Paralipomena: Kleine philosophische
Schriften, Vol. 2 (Berlin: Hahn, 1851), Chapter 11,
"Nachträge zur Lehre von der Nichtigkeit des Daseyns,"
§147, 245–246, Translated by Wilhelm Snyman, 2016

The meaning and the quality of life

The unfortunateness of our lives is not limited to the absence of cosmic (and the dearth of terrestrial) meaning. It is also attributable, as I argue in this chapter, to the dismal quality of our lives. Both the deficiency of meaning and the poor quality of life are features of the human predicament.

This formulation suggests that meaning and quality are two entirely distinct features of the human predicament. However, it is also possible to view meaning as a component of a life's quality. Either way, there is heuristic value in considering them separately because meaning in life, a key existential issue, is, at the very most, only *one* component of the quality of life, and it is helpful to consider the other components separately.

The precise relationship between the meaning and the quality of life depends on how one understands the respective concepts and what view one takes about what makes a life meaningful and what makes a life good.

Whatever view one takes about whether life *actually* is meaningful, *feeling* that one's life is meaningful contributes toward enhancing life's quality, and *feeling* that one's life is meaningless contributes toward reducing the quality of life. Life feels better if it feels meaningful, and a perception that one's life is meaningless can have deep and widespread negative effects on the quality of life.

However, on at least some views, a life can have great (terrestrial) meaning despite the life's quality being poor. The incarceration of Nelson Mandela, for example, radically reduced the quality of his life, but in time, it added immense meaning. It is a cruel irony that meaning in life can actually be enhanced by events that cause a reduction in (other aspects of) the quality of life, as was arguably the case with Mr. Mandela. His imprisonment and the associated hardships and indignities—and his response to them—made him a more potent symbol than he would have been had he escaped from South Africa and lived through the remainder of the apartheid period in exile, with a higher quality of life overall.

It is also possible, on some views, for a meaningless life to rate (relatively) highly in (other aspects of) the quality-of-life scale. The meaningless life of a jet-setting playboy millionaire might be regarded as a life of high quality (by some). All other things being equal, it certainly is not among the most miserable of human lives.

One interesting connection between the meaning and the quality of life is that questions of meaning often arise when life is going badly. You are in a serious accident, or your child dies, or you are diagnosed with cancer. You then ask: "What is it all about?" or "Why me?" People do not tend to ask the same questions in response to things going (relatively) well.[1] If you win the lottery, you might well marvel at your luck, but you do not spend nights lying awake and reflecting on that luck and wondering why you of all people should have won the lottery. Even when both the good and the bad are mere dumb luck, it is the bad that precipitates the gnawing questions.

Of course, questions about meaning also arise in those whose quality of life is otherwise relatively good, but it is the bad rather than the good things in life that tend to precipitate the search for meaning. The playboy millionaire might eventually pause to wonder whether his life is meaningless. However, that is likely due to something bad about the quality of his life—advancing age or some other reminder of his mortality.

The quality of life is a feature of the human predicament not only because it leads to questions about life's meaning, but also in its own right. The quality of human life is, contrary to what many people think, actually quite appalling.

The quality of people's lives obviously varies immensely. However, thinking that some lives are worse or better than others is merely a comparative claim. It tells us nothing about whether the worse lives are bad enough to count as bad lives or whether the better lives are good enough to count as good lives. The common view, however, is that the quality of some lives qualifies as bad and the quality of others qualifies as good. In contrast to this view, I believe that while some lives are better than others, none are (noncomparatively or objectively) good.

The obvious objection to this view is that billions of people judge the quality of their own lives to be good. How can it possibly be argued that they are mistaken and that the quality of their lives is, in fact, bad?

The response to this objection consists of two main steps. The first is to demonstrate that people are very unreliable judges of the quality of their own lives. The second step is to show that when we correct for the biases that explain the unreliability of these assessments and we look at human lives more accurately, we find that the quality (of even the best lives) is actually very poor.

Why people's judgments about the quality of their lives are unreliable

People's self-assessments of wellbeing are unreliable indicators of quality of life because these self-assessments are influenced by three psychological phenomena, the existence of which has been well demonstrated.

The first of these is an optimism bias, sometimes known as Pollyannaism. For example, when asked to rate how happy they are, people's responses are disproportionately toward the happier end of the spectrum. Only a small minority of people rate themselves as "not too happy."[2] When people are asked to rate their wellbeing relative to others, the typical response is that they are doing better than the "most commonly experienced level," suggesting, in the words of two authors, "an interesting bias in perception."[3] It is unsurprising that people's reports of their overall wellbeing is unduly optimistic, because the building blocks of that judgment are similarly prone to an optimism bias. For example, people are (excessively) optimistic in their projections of what will happen to them in the future.[4] The findings regarding recall of past experiences are more complicated.[5] However, the dominant finding, subject to some qualifications,[6] seems to be that there is greater recall of positive experiences than there is of negative ones. This may be because negative experiences are susceptible to cognitive processes that suppress them. Judgments about the overall quality of one's life that are inadequately informed by the bad things that have happened and will happen are not reliable judgments.

There is ample evidence of an optimism bias among humans. This is not to say that the extent of the bias does not vary a lot. The inhabitants of some countries report greater subjective wellbeing than those of other countries even when the objective conditions are similar.[7] This has been attributed, in part, to cultural variation.[8] However, optimism bias is found everywhere even though the extent of the bias varies.[9]

A second psychological phenomenon that should lead to skepticism about self-assessments of wellbeing is known variously as accommodation, adaptation, or habituation. If one's self-assessments were reliable, they would track improvements and deteriorations in one's objective conditions. That is to say, if one's condition improved or deteriorated, one would perceive one's condition to have improved or deteriorated to that degree.

Self-assessment would then remain fixed until there was a further improvement or deterioration, in response to which one's self-assessment would also adjust.

However, that is not what happens. Our subjective assessments *do* respond to shifts in our objective conditions, but the altered self-assessment is not stable. As we adjust to our new condition, we cease to rate our condition as we did when it first improved or deteriorated. For example, if one suddenly loses the use of both legs, one's subjective assessment will drop precipitously. In time, however, subjective assessment of quality of life will improve as one adjusts to the paralysis. One's objective condition will not have improved—the paralysis remains—but one will judge life to be going less badly than immediately after the paralysis.[10]

There is some disagreement about the extent to which we adapt. Some have suggested that it is complete—that we return to a baseline or "setpoint" level of subjective wellbeing. Others deny that the evidence shows this, at least not in every domain of our lives.[11] However, there is no dispute that there is some adaptation and that it is sometimes significant. This is all that is required to lend support to the claim that our subjective assessments are unreliable.

The third feature of human psychology that compromises the reliability of subjective assessments of wellbeing is what we might call "comparison." Subjective assessments of wellbeing implicitly involve comparison with the wellbeing of others.[12] Our judgments about the quality of our own lives are influenced by the (perceived) quality of the lives of others. One consequence of this is that bad features of all human lives are substantially overlooked in judging the quality of one's life. Because these features of one's life are no worse than those of other humans, we tend to omit them in reaching a judgment about the quality of our own life.

Whereas Pollyannaism biases judgments only in the optimistic direction, adaptation and comparison are more complicated. One adapts not only to deteriorations but also to improvements in one's objective condition. Similarly, one can compare oneself not only to those worse off than oneself but also to those better off than oneself. It would be a mistake, however, to think that the net effect is to cancel any bias. This is because both adaptation and comparison work against the backdrop of the optimism bias. They may moderate the optimism bias, but they do not cancel it. Moreover, there is an optimism bias in the manifestation of these other traits. For example, we are more likely to compare ourselves with those who are worse off than with those who are better off.[13] For these reasons, the net effect of the three traits is for us to overestimate the actual quality of our lives.

The vast body of evidence for these psychological characteristics of humans is simply undeniable. This is not to say that *every* human overestimates the quality of his or her life. The evidence shows that the phenomenon is widespread—but not universal. There are some people who have accurate assessments, but these are the minority and very likely include those who do not take issue with my grim view about the quality of human life.

This is not to say that subjective assessments are irrelevant. Thinking that one's life is better than it actually is *can* make it better than it would otherwise be. In other words, there can be a feedback loop whereby a positive subjective assessment actually improves one's objective wellbeing. However, there is a difference between a subjective assessment of one's wellbeing *influencing* the objective level and a subjective assessment *determining* the objective level. Even if an overly optimistic subjective assessment makes one's life better than it would otherwise be, it does not follow that one's life is actually going as well as one thinks it is.

I have shown so far that there is excellent reason to distrust cheery subjective assessments about the quality of human life. However, to show that the quality of people's lives is worse than they think it is, is not to show that the quality of their lives is very bad. That conclusion requires further argument, which I now provide.

The poor quality of human life

Most people recognize that human lives can sometimes be of an appallingly low quality. The tendency, however, is to think that this is true of *other people's* lives, not one's own. When people do think their own lives are of low quality, this is typically because their lives are in fact unusually bad. However, if we look dispassionately at human life and control for our biases, we find that all human life is permeated by badness.

Even in good health, much of every day is spent in discomfort. Within hours, we become thirsty and hungry. Many millions of people are chronically hungry. When we can access food and beverage and thus succeed in warding off hunger and thirst for a while, we then come to feel the discomfort of distended bladders and bowels. Sometimes, relief can be obtained relatively easily, but on other occasions, the opportunity for (dignified[14]) relief is not as forthcoming as we would like. We also spend much of our time in thermal discomfort—feeling either too hot or too cold. Unless one naps at the first sign of weariness, one spends quite a bit of the day feeling tired. Indeed, many people wake up tired and spend the day in that state.

With the exception of *chronic* hunger among the world's poor, these discomforts all tend to be dismissed as minor matters. While they are minor relative to the other bad things that befall people, they are not inconsequential. A blessed species that never experienced these discomforts would rightly note that if we take discomfort to be bad, then we should take the daily discomforts that humans experience more seriously than we do.

Other negative states are experienced regularly even if not daily or by everybody. Itches and allergies are common. Minor illnesses like colds are suffered by almost everybody. For some people, this happens multiple times a year. For others, it occurs annually or every few years. Many women of reproductive years suffer regular menstrual pains and menopausal women suffer hot flashes.[15] Conditions such as nausea, hypoglycemia, seizures, and chronic pain are widespread.

The negative features of life are not just restricted to unpleasant physical sensations. For example, we frequently encounter frustrations and irritations. We have to wait in traffic or stand in lines. We encounter inefficiency, stupidity, evil, Byzantine bureaucracies, and other obstacles that can take thousands of hours to overcome—if they can be overcome at all. Many important aspirations are unfulfilled. Millions of people seek jobs but remain unemployed. Of those who have jobs, many are dissatisfied with them, or even loathe them. Even those who enjoy their work may have professional aspirations that remain unfulfilled. Most people yearn for close and rewarding personal relationships, not least with a lifelong partner or spouse. For some, this desire is never fulfilled. For others, it temporarily is, but then they find that the relationship is trying and stultifying, or their partner betrays them or becomes exploitative or abusive. Most people are unhappy in some or other way with their appearance—they are too fat, or they are too short, or their ears are too big. People want to be, look, and feel younger, and yet they age relentlessly. They have high hopes for their children and these are often thwarted when, for example, the children prove to be a disappointment in some way or other. When those close to us suffer, we suffer at the sight of it. When they die, we are bereft.

We are vulnerable to innumerable appalling fates. Although each fate does not befall every one of us, our very existence puts us at risk for these outcomes, and the cumulative risk of something horrific occurring to each one of us is simply enormous. If we include death, as I argue in the next chapter that we ought to do, then the risk is in fact a certainty,

Burn victims, for example, suffer excruciating pain, not only in the moment but also for years thereafter. The wound itself is obviously painful, but the treatment intensifies and protracts the pain. One such victim describes his daily "bath" in a disinfectant that would sting intact skin but causes unspeakable pain where there is little or no skin. The bandages stick to the flesh and removing them, which can take an hour or more if the burns are extensive, causes indescribable pain.[16] Repeated surgery can be required, but even with the best treatment, the victim is left with lifelong disfigurement and the social and psychological difficulties associated with it.

Consider next those who are quadriplegic or, worse still, suffer from locked-in syndrome. This is sheer mental torture. One eloquent amyotrophic lateral sclerosis sufferer describes this disease as "progressive imprisonment without parole"[17] because of the advancing and irreversible paralysis. Dictating an essay at the point when he had become quadriplegic, and before losing the ability to speak, he describes his torments, which are most acute at night. When he is put to bed, he has to have his limbs placed in exactly the position he wants them for the night. He says that if he allows "a stray limb to be misplaced" or "fail to insist on having [his] midriff carefully aligned with legs and head," he will "suffer the agonies of the damned later in the night."[18] He invites us to consider how often we shift and move during the course of a night, and he says that "enforced stillness for hours on end is not only physically uncomfortable but psychologically close to intolerable."[19] He lies on his back in a semi-upright position, attached to a breathing device and left alone with his thoughts. Unable to move, any itch must go unscratched. His condition, he says, is one of "humiliating helplessness."[20]

Cancer's reputation as a dreaded disease is well deserved. There is much suffering in dying from this disease, but at least as much in the treatments that are usually necessary to cure the patient of the malignancy. In the worst scenarios, the patient suffers from both the treatment and its failure.

When symptoms have not precipitated the diagnosis, the first blow is the diagnosis itself. Arthur Frank says that on receiving the news that he had a malignancy, he felt as though his "body had become a quicksand" in which he was sinking.[21] But that is only the beginning. For example, radiation treatment for esophageal cancel left Christopher Hitchens desperately attempting to avoid the inevitable need to swallow. Every time he did swallow, "a hellish tide of pain would flow up [his] throat, culminating in what felt like a mule kick in the small of [his] back."[22] Ruth Rakoff, after receiving chemotherapy for breast cancer, described her "insides as raw."[23] Treatment can result in nausea, vomiting, constipation, diarrhea, and gum and dental soreness. Food tastes bad and appetite is lost. Unsurprisingly, all this results in weight loss and fatigue. Neuropathy is another common side effect, as is hair loss. Many of the same symptoms can be experienced even in the absence of treatment or after treatment has been ended. Moreover, tumors pressing on brains, bowels, and bones can cause excruciating pain. When the pain can be controlled, it is sometimes at the expense of consciousness or at least lucidity.

Cancer is an appalling fate, but it is also a common one (in those countries where people do not typically die earlier of infectious diseases). In the United States, it has been estimated that one in two men and one in three women will develop cancer, and one in four men and one in five women will die from it.[24] It has recently been suggested that estimates of lifetime risk of developing cancer may be exaggerated by the fact that some people develop cancer more than once. However, even if we opt for the more conservative estimate of lifetime risk of first primary, we find that 40% of men and 37% of women in the United Kingdom will develop cancer.[25] Those who do not get cancer are still at risk for hundreds of other possible causes of suffering.

It is, of course, more commonly, older people who get cancer.[26] However, although it is, all things being equal, generally worse to die when one is younger than when one is older,[27] the physical and psychological symptoms of life with cancer and dying from cancer are no less appalling at older ages.

Pain accompanies many conditions, but we should remember that much of it is not attendant upon visible conditions. It is often hidden from those not experiencing it. One sufferer from chronic pain describes it as "debilitating" and observes that it "can take over one's life, sap one's energy, and negate or neutralize joy and well-being."[28]

Not all suffering is physical, although psychological ailments can certainly have bodily symptoms. William Styron, describing his depression, said that ultimately, "the body is affected and feels sapped, drained."[29] He wrote of his "slowed-down responses, near paralysis, psychic energy throttled back close to zero."[30] Sleep is disrupted, with the sufferer staring "up into yawning darkness, wondering and writhing at the devastation"[31] of his mind. The sufferer from depression, we are told, is "like a walking casualty of war."[32]

In addition, there is an atrociously diverse range of harms that people suffer at the hands of other humans, including being betrayed, humiliated, shamed, denigrated, maligned, beaten, assaulted, raped, kidnapped, abducted, tortured, and murdered.[33]

The horrors of each could be enumerated but consider those of rape as an example. Rape[34] can instill terror in the victim before and while she or he is violated. Physical injury, including bruising and laceration, is not an uncommon consequence of the assault. There can be lifelong psychological repercussions, including rage, shame, feelings of worthlessness, and difficulties with intimacy. A pregnancy can result if the victim is a fertile female. Even when abortions are freely available, there can be psychic trauma in terminating the pregnancy. Carrying the fetus to term can be even more psychologically distressing. Rape victims can also contract sexually transmitted diseases from their assailants. These in turn have many harmful physical effects and can cause great mental trauma as well.

Why there is more bad than good

Optimists will very likely suggest that this is a one-sided picture—that lives typically contain not only bad but also good. However, although it is true that lives are not usually *unadulteratedly* bad, there is much more bad than good even for the luckiest humans. Things are worse still for unluckier people, many of whom have almost nothing going in their favor.

Our lives contain so much more bad than good in part because of a series of empirical differences between bad things and good things. For example, the most intense pleasures are short-lived, whereas the worst pains can be much more enduring. Orgasms, for example, pass quickly. Gastronomic pleasures last a bit longer, but even if the pleasure of good food is protracted, it lasts no more than a few hours. Severe pains can endure for days, months, and years. Indeed, pleasures in general—not just the most sublime of them—tend to be shorter-lived than pains. Chronic pain is rampant, but there is no such thing as chronic pleasure. There are people who have an enduring sense of contentment or satisfaction, but that is not the same as chronic pleasure. Moreover, *dis*content and *dis*satisfaction can be as enduring as contentment and satisfaction; this means that the positive states are not advantaged in this realm. Indeed, the positive states are less stable because it is much easier for things to go wrong than to go right.

The worst pains are also worse than the best pleasures are good. Those who deny this should consider whether they would accept an hour of the most delightful pleasures in exchange for an hour of the worst tortures. Arthur Schopenhauer makes a similar point when he asks us to "compare the respective feelings of two animals, one of which is engaged in eating the other."[35] The animal being eaten suffers and loses vastly more than the animal that is eating gains from this one meal.

Consider too the temporal dimensions of injury or illness and recovery. One can be injured in seconds: One is hit by a bullet or projectile, or is knocked over or falls, or suffers a stroke or heart attack. In these and other ways, one can instantly lose one's sight or hearing or the use of a limb or years of learning. The path to recovery is slow. In many cases, full recovery is never attained. Injury comes in an instant, but the resultant suffering can last a lifetime. Even lesser injuries and illnesses are typically incurred much more quickly than one recovers from them. For example, the common cold strikes quickly and is defeated much more slowly by one's immune system. The symptoms manifest with increasing intensity within hours, but they take at least days, if not weeks, to disappear entirely.

There are, of course, conditions in which one declines gradually rather than suddenly, but the great majority of these—including age-related physical decline, dementia, neuromuscular degenerative diseases, and the deterioration from advancing cancers—are conditions from which there is no recovery. Where there are treatments, some are merely palliative. When treatments are potentially curative, the decline is the default against which one has to battle, sometimes successfully but other times not. Moreover, billions of people simply have no access to either curative or palliative treatments.

We should not think that gradual declines are restricted to diseases. Gradual decline is actually a feature that characterizes most of normal human life. After the growth of infancy and childhood,[36] the normal human flowers in very young adulthood. (In some ways, the peak is just before adolescence, which wreaks all kinds of havoc.) Thereafter, from one's early twenties and on, one begins the long, slow decline. Some of the mental decline is masked and counteracted by hard work or by increasing wisdom. Thus, at least in some areas of pursuit (but not others), people do not reach their professional or overall mental peaks until later in life. However, there is an underlying decline, at least physically and to some extent also mentally: Hair turns gray or begins to fall out; wrinkles begin to appear and various body parts sag; muscle gives way to fat, as strength does to weakness; and eyesight and hearing begin to fail.[37]

This long decline characterizes the majority of one's life. At first, the decline is imperceptible, but then it becomes all too evident. If, for example, one views photographs of a person taken over the course of his or her life, one cannot but be struck by the deterioration. The strong, vibrant youth gradually makes way for the weak, decrepit ancient. It is not an uplifting series of images. Some might suggest that the decline is not so bad in the earlier stages. They are obviously right that it is not as bad as it gets later, but that does not mean that the decline is absent. Moreover, it clearly bothers many people—and not only those who resort to various cosmetic interventions such as dyeing their hair, injecting Botox, and surgery.

Things are also stacked against us in the fulfillment of our desires and the satisfaction of our preferences.[38] Many of our desires are never fulfilled. There are thus more unfulfilled than fulfilled desires. Even when desires are fulfilled, they are not fulfilled immediately. Thus, there is a period during which those desires remain unfulfilled. Sometimes, that is a relatively short period (such as between thirst and, in ordinary circumstances, its quenching), but in the case of more ambitious desires, they can take months, years, or decades to fulfill. Some desires that are fulfilled prove less satisfying than we had imagined. One wants a specific job or to marry a particular person, but upon attaining one's goal, one learns that the job is less interesting or the spouse is more irritating than one thought.

Even when fulfilled desires are everything that they were expected to be, the satisfaction is typically transitory, as the fulfilled desires yield to new desires. Sometimes, the new desires are more of the same. For example, one eats to satiety but then hunger gradually sets in again and one desires more food. The "treadmill of desires" works in another way too. When one can regularly satisfy one's lower-level desires, a new and more demanding level of desires emerges. Thus, those who cannot provide for their own basic needs spend their time striving to fulfill these. Those who can satisfy the recurring basic needs develop what Abraham Maslow calls a "higher discontent"[39] that they seek to satisfy. When that level of desires can be satisfied, the aspirations shift to a yet higher level.

Life is thus a constant state of striving. There are sometimes reprieves, but the striving ends only with the end of life. Moreover, as should be obvious, the striving is to ward off bad things and attain good things. Indeed, some of the good things amount merely to the temporary relief from the bad things. For example, one satisfies one's hunger or quenches one's thirst. Notice too that while the bad things come without any effort, one has to strive to ward them off and attain the good things. Ignorance, for example, is effortless, but knowledge usually requires hard work.

Even the extent to which our desires and goals are fulfilled creates a misleadingly optimistic impression of how well our lives are going. This is because there is actually a form of self "censorship" in the formulation of our desires and goals. While many of them are never fulfilled, there are many more potential desires and goals that we do not even formulate because we know that they are unattainable. For example, we know that we cannot live for a few hundred years and that we cannot gain expertise in all the subjects in which we are interested. Thus, we set goals that are less unrealistic (even if many of them are nonetheless somewhat optimistic). Thus, one hopes to live a life that is, by human standards, a long life, and we hope to gain expertise in some, perhaps very focused, area. What this means is that, even if all our desires and goals were fulfilled, our lives are not going as well as they would be going if the formulation of our desires had not been artificially restricted.

Further insight into the poor quality of human life can be gained from considering various traits that are often thought to be components of a good life and by noting what limited quantities of these characterize even the best human lives. For example, knowledge and understanding are widely thought to be goods, and people are often in awe of how much knowledge and understanding (some) humans have. The sad truth, however, is that, on the spectrum from no knowledge and understanding to omniscience, even the cleverest, best-educated humans are much closer to the unfortunate end of the spectrum.[40] There are billions more things we do not know or understand than we do know and understand. If knowledge really is a good thing and we have so little of it, our lives are not going very well in this regard.

Similarly, we consider longevity to be a good thing (at least if the life is above a minimum quality threshold[41]). Yet even the longest human lives are ultimately fleeting. If we think that longevity is a good thing, then a life of a thousand years (in full vigor) would be much better than a life of eighty or ninety years (especially when the last few decades are years of decline and decrepitude). Ninety years are much closer to one year than to a thousand years. It is even more distant from two thousand or three thousand or more. If, all things being equal, longer lives are better than shorter ones, human lives do not fare well at all.[42]

It is not surprising that we fail to notice this heavy preponderance of bad in human life. The facts I have described are deep and intractable features of human (and other) life. Most humans have accommodated to the human condition and thus fail to notice just how bad it is. Their expectations and evaluations are rooted in this unfortunate baseline. Longevity, for example, is judged relative to the longest actual human lifespans and not relative to an ideal standard. The same is true of knowledge, understanding, moral goodness, and aesthetic appreciation. Similarly, we expect recovery to take longer than injury, and thus we judge the quality of human life off that baseline, even though it is an appalling fact of life that the odds are stacked against us in this and other ways.

The psychological trait of comparison is obviously also a factor. Because the negative features I have described are common to all lives, they play very little role in how people assess the quality of their lives. It is true for everybody that the worst pains are worse than the best pleasures are good, and that pains can and often do last much longer than pleasures. Everybody must work hard to ward off unpleasantness and seek the good things. Thus, when people judge the quality of their own lives and do so by comparing them to the lives of others, they tend to overlook these and other such features.

All this occurs against the backdrop of an optimism bias, under which we are already inclined to focus on the good more than the bad. The fact that we fail to notice how bad human life is does not detract from the arguments I have given that there is much more bad than good. Human life would be vastly better if pain were fleeting and pleasure protracted; if the pleasures were much better than the pains were bad; if it were really difficult to be injured or get sick; if recovery were swift when injury or illness did befall us; and if our desires were fulfilled instantly and if they did not give way to new desires. Human life would also be immensely better if we lived for many thousands of years in good health and if we were much wiser, cleverer, and morally better than we are.[43]

Secular optimistic theodicies

Human optimism is resilient. It does not wilt in the face of evidence. No matter how much evidence one provides for psychological traits such as optimism bias, and no matter how much evidence there is that the quality of human life is very bad, most humans will adhere to their optimistic views. Sometimes, this optimism manifests, at least in part, as religious faith,[44] with people declaring the goodness of God and his creations. Religious optimism of this kind is often challenged by the "argument from evil," which suggests that the existence of an omniscient, omnipotent, omnibenevolent God is incompatible with the vast amount of evil that exists in the world. Theodicy is the optimistic practice of trying to reconcile God's existence with that evil. However, many atheists, while critical of theodicy, are themselves engaged in a kind of secular theodicy—an attempt to reconcile their optimistic views with the unfortunate facts about the human condition.

There are many secular theodicies. One of the most commonly expressed is that the bad things in life are necessary. For example, it is suggested that, without pain, we would incur more injuries. Indeed, those people with congenital insensitivity to pain harm themselves unwittingly by, for example, grasping and continuing to hold objects that are dangerously hot, or by unrestricted use of limbs in which a bone has been broken. In the absence of pain, they are simply not alerted to the danger.

It is also suggested that the bad things in life are necessary in order to appreciate the good things, or at least to appreciate them fully. On this view, we can only enjoy pleasures (as much as we do) because we also experience pain. Similarly, our achievements are more satisfying if we have to work hard to attain them, and fulfilled desires mean more to us because we know that desires are not always fulfilled.

There are many problems with this sort of argument. First, these sorts of claims are not always true. There is much pain that serves no useful purpose. There is no value in labor pains or in pain resulting from terminal diseases, for example. While the pain associated with kidney stones might now lead somebody to seek medical help, for most of human history, such pain served no purpose, as there was absolutely nothing anybody could do about kidney stones.[45] Moreover, there are at least some pleasures we can enjoy without having to experience pain. Pleasant tastes, for example, do not require any experience of pain or unpleasantness. Similarly, many achievements can be satisfying even if they involve less or no striving. There may be a special satisfaction in the ease of attainment. There may be some individual variation. Perhaps some people are more capable of enjoying pleasure without having to experience pain and more capable of taking satisfaction in achievements that come with ease.

Second, insofar as the good things in life do require a contrast in order to be fully appreciated, it is not clear that this appreciation requires as much bad as there is. We do not, for example, require millions of people suffering from chronic pain, infectious diseases, advancing paralysis, and tumors in order to appreciate the good things in life. We could enjoy our achievements without having to work quite so hard to attain them.

Finally, and perhaps most important, to the extent that the bad things in life really are necessary, our lives are worse than they would be if the bad things were not necessary. There are both real and conceivable beings in which nociceptive (that is, specialized neural) pathways detect and transmit noxious stimuli, resulting in avoidance without being mediated by pain. This is true of plants and simple animal organisms, and it is also true of the reflex arc in more complex animals, such as humans.[46] We can also imagine beings much more rational than humans, in which nociception and aversive behavior were mediated by a rational faculty rather than a capacity to feel pain. In such beings, a noxious stimulus would be received but not felt (or at least not in the way pain is), and the rational faculty would, as reliably as pain, induce the being to withdraw. It would be much better to be that sort of being than to be our sort of being. It would similarly be better to be the sort of being who can appreciate the good things in life without having to experience bad things or without having to work really hard to attain the good things. Lives in which there is "no gain without pain"[47] are much worse than lives in which there could be "the same gain without pain."

A second theodicy picks up here. It insists that the perfectionist standards I am using to judge the quality of human life are too demanding and not appropriate. One version of this critique says that we must adopt a human perspective, not the so-called perspective of the universe, in determining what is good for humans.[48] Now, of course, there is a sense in which it is true that we need to take account of what sort of beings humans are in order to determine what is good for them. For example, given that we are terrestrial animals, submerging a human underwater (without breathing equipment) is going to be bad for that human even though it would not be bad for a fish. Yet we can say that it would certainly be better for humans if they could not drown (that is, if they had the capacity to breathe not only in air but also in water).

Here, another version of the second theodicy is often invoked. It claims that there are constraints on how good a human life can be while still being a human life. A being that could breathe not only in air but also underwater would not be a human. A life without pain would not be a human life. Nor should we judge the extent of human knowledge, understanding, and goodness by the standards of omniscience and omnibenevolence, because the latter standards are not human standards. An omniscient, omnibenevolent being would not be a human. It would be God.

This version of the argument is also unconvincing. The problem is that it fetishizes human life. Some emotional distance might be required to realize this and thus consider an imaginary species rather than humans. Members of this fictional species, which we might call *Homo infortunatus*, have an even more wretched quality of life than most humans have, but their lives are not devoid of all pleasure and other goods. Now imagine that a pessimistic philosopher among them observes how appalling their lives are. He points to how much better things could be. For example, instead of living only thirty years, they might live to eighty or ninety. Instead of being in an almost constant state of hunger, they might get hungry only between three regular meals a day. Instead of being sick every week, they might suffer illness only annually or even less often. In response to such observations, the optimistic members of the species—a vast majority—would object that if their lives were better in those ways, they would no longer be *infortunati*. That observation, even if true, would not detract from the claim that the quality of life of the *infortunati* is wretched. There is, after all, a difference between asking how good the quality of life of a particular species is and asking whether a much better life is compatible with being a member of that species. Perhaps we would not be human if the quality of our lives were *much* better than it is. It does not follow that the quality of human life is good.

To prefer a human life to a better life—in a choice that is currently hypothetical but might someday be actual—suggests a distracting sentimentality about humanity. It is to think that it is more important to be human than to have a better quality of life. Yet the typical reasons provided for the value of being human rather than some other species seem to imply that it would be better to be better than to be human, even if that implication is not typically noticed. For example, most humans think that it is better to have the higher cognitive capacity of *Homo sapiens* than the lesser capacity of *Homo erectus*. It seems that the logic underlying this judgment is that greater cognitive capacity is better than lesser cognitive capacity. But this logic supports a further judgment that it would be better to have the still-greater cognitive capacity of a superhuman species.

One way to ward off this implication would be to claim that there is a "Goldilocks" level of cognitive capacity. On this view, it is bad to have too little but also bad to have too much. (Perhaps too much cognitive capacity either gives one insights that are conducive to unhappiness or can lead to unacceptable levels of destructiveness.) The problem with the Goldilocks argument is that, if there is some optimum level of cognitive sophistication, it is both too convenient and implausible to think that the level is that of *Homo sapiens*.

It is difficult to prove this to those who take it as an article of faith that humans have the optimum level of this trait. However, consider that humans' greater cognitive capacity has led them to be much more destructive than their fellow hominids and other primates. Yet humans lack the still-further sophistication that would check that destructiveness by, for example, enabling them to think and act more rationally. Perhaps it will be argued in response that although humans would become less destructive if they were cognitively more sophisticated, they would acquire, with that greater cognitive capacity, unbearable insight into the human predicament, thereby making them unhappier. But humans do suffer a great deal from such angst, which suggests that they may already have too much cognitive capacity for their own happiness.

I have referred to cognitive capacity as a trait. It is, however, a constellation of traits. As implausible as it is to claim that humans possess the optimum degree of cognitive capacity overall, it is still less plausible to make this claim with respect to some of the component capacities. Think of computational ability, for example. It would be better if ordinary humans had greater computational ability than they currently have, at least if this did not involve a reduction in any other capacities.

It is even harder to argue that humans occupy a Goldilocks position on the spectra of other attributes. For example, it would be exceedingly difficult to defend the view that humans have an optimum degree of moral goodness, as this would imply that it would be worse if they were morally better. If this is not absurd, it is at least highly implausible.

Not all optimists fetishize humanity. Among the advocates of human enhancement are those who envisage and welcome the prospect of a "post-human" future—a future in which humans have been so enhanced (physically, mentally, and morally) that they are no longer recognizably human. These advocates of trans-humanism think it is much more important to improve the quality of life than for the enhanced future beings to be human.

Although there are many who object to the wisdom and morality of seeking such enhancements, I am not among those categorically opposed to technological enhancements. If the choice is between a lower quality of life and a higher quality of life, the latter is preferable even if the enhanced beings with the better quality lives can no longer be categorized as humans. To be sure, any enhancements will need to be subject to the usual moral constraints. For example, enhancements that carry significant risks of causing serious harm might fall afoul of such constraints. And attention would need to be paid to fair access to enhancement technologies. None of this, however, rules out the transhumanist project.

However, while transhumanists are not fixated on whether a life is human, they are nonetheless engaged in another kind of secular optimistic theodicy. They believe that the enhancements that will become possible will improve the quality of life sufficiently that life will be not merely better but good. We might say they have faith in the "salvific" or "redemptive" powers of enhancement. Humans may not have "fallen," but they are nonetheless low. The good news, though, on this view, is that things can get much better in a future "messianic" era of enhancement.[49]

When this view is criticized as being too optimistic, the criticism is usually that the hoped-for enhancements are unlikely to be achievable (or achievable within the projected timeframe[50]). The suggestion is that advocates of enhancement have an exaggerated view about what kinds of enhancement will be possible. According to this criticism, it is naïvely optimistic to think, for example, that major lifespan extension is possible or that human cognitive capacities could be radically enhanced.

Even if we assume, however, that transhumanism is not overly optimistic in this regard, it is unduly optimistic in another way. It assumes that the quality of life after the anticipated enhancements would be good (enough). This assumption is problematic. While the quality of life would be *better*, it is not clear that it would be good enough to count as good.[51] For example, it would be better to live much longer in good health, and it would be better if we knew much more than we do, but even lives enhanced in these and other ways would be far from ideal. We would still die, and we would still have vastly more ignorance than knowledge.[52]

The relative force of the two charges of optimism is interactive. The more ambitious the claims about what improvements can be made, the more susceptible these claims are to the first kind of objection—namely, that the projections are overly optimistic. On the other hand, the more modest the claims are about what can be achieved, the more susceptible the view is to the charge that enhancement is merely a mollification of life's harshness and not the promise of Eden.

Conclusion

The optimistic delusions to which humans are prone do make the quality of human life a little less bad than it otherwise would be. In this way, they partially palliate the human predicament—or at least they do so for those who have them. The quality of life just does not feel quite as bad as it would in the absence of the rose-colored glasses. I shall say more in the concluding chapter about whether this supports an argument for an optimistic response to the human predicament. For now, we need note only that to palliate a predicament is not to elude it. Even armed with various optimistic coping mechanisms, the quality of human life is not only much worse than most people think but actually quite awful. This may not be true in every minute or even hour of (human) life—there are moments of relief and pleasure—but taken as a whole, it is an unenviable condition.

5 | Death

> *Vita nostra brevis est*
> *Brevi finietur.*
> *Venit mors velociter*
> *Rapit nos atrociter*
> *Nemini parcetur.*
>
> Our life is brief
> Soon it will end.
> Death comes quickly
> Snatches us cruelly
> To nobody shall it be spared.
> —*De Brevitate Vitae (Gaudeamus igitur)*

Introduction

It would be an understatement of immense proportions to say that humans are averse to their own deaths.* The prospect of death terrifies many, but an even larger number of people expend a great deal of energy warding it off. Admittedly some of this energy is directed toward intermediate goals, such as nourishment and hydration, the attainment of which people find independently

---

*This is by far the longest chapter in the book. Those who prefer a shorter reading should consult "A Reader's Guide" at the beginning of the book for suggestions of what may be skipped.

satisfying, but which also have the effect of keeping death at bay. It is entirely unsurprising, given our evolutionary history, that we find many means of death avoidance to be rewarding.

Other evolutionarily engrained instincts of life preservation are not mediated by such explicit rewards. We navigate the archipelago of life's perils, sometimes consciously and sometimes unconsciously. For example, we pay attention to and avoid getting in the path of moving vehicles as we cross roads; we recoil from snakes and duck in order to evade gunfire and other projectiles; we run from burning houses; and we do not walk off the edges of cliffs.

The aversion to death is not mere instinct. When people are explicitly asked, they typically say that death is a fate that they are extremely keen to prevent. So great is the ordinary aversion to death that it will often be avoided even when great costs are attached to that evasion. Although death is a release from innumerable living hells to which humans are vulnerable, it is remarkable how resistant humans typically are to death even when that aversion perpetuates their misery. When somebody (eventually) decides that release is preferable, he or she usually continues to regard death as the lesser of two evils. That is to say, death is not *wanted*, but it is the only available means to what *is* wanted, namely, the release from the horrors of continued existence.

That people can and do reach this point shows that, at least for many, death is not the *worst* of fates. It is nonetheless regarded as a terrible one. It is also the *certain* fate of each of us. Benjamin Franklin once remarked, presumably in jest, that "in this world, nothing can be certain, except death and taxes."[1] He was only half right. There are tax havens, but there are unfortunately no death havens—no places where one can hide from death. This is especially unfortunate because however much people complain about taxes, death is significantly worse. Each one of us is going to die and we live our lives knowing this. We have no control over the fact that we shall die. One can choose to hasten (or not delay) one's death, in which case, one can sometimes also choose the means of one's death. However, one cannot choose not to die.

The certain prospect of death dooms us to destruction. That makes death sound like a part of the human predicament. Some might wonder how that could be so if, as I have argued, the human predicament includes the poor quality of human life and our cosmic insignificance. If living a life of that kind is a predicament, why is the end of that life not deliverance from the predicament?

One reason is the intractability of real predicaments, of which the human predicament may well be the paradigmatic example. If one is in a predicament from which there is a costless (or a low-cost) escape, one is not really in a predicament. If, for example, one is up a creek without a paddle but one does have an outboard motor, then being up a creek without a paddle is not a real predicament. Real predicaments—the wrenching ones—are those in which there is no easy solution. Death might deliver us from suffering, but annihilation, as I shall argue, is an extremely costly "solution" and thus only deepens the predicament.

And death does not solve the problem of our cosmic meaninglessness. Indeed, as I argued in chapter 3, the fact that we die contributes to that meaninglessness. If one were immortal, there would be no need to seek a purpose that survived one's personal extinction. With death we cease to be, but we do not thereby cease to be cosmically insignificant.

Moreover, insofar as our lives *are* meaningful, that meaning is usually threatened by one's own death and the deaths of those fellow terrestrials from whose perspective one's life has meaning.

For example, if one's life has some meaning because of one's relationships with family and friends, then death typically threatens this meaning by preventing the continuation of those relationships. Similarly, meaning derived from teaching the young, treating the sick, creating art, or advancing science cannot continue to be generated once one dies for the obvious reason that death prevents one from continuing these activities. Residue of the meaning created during one's life might persist for a while, in the memories of and ongoing effects on those who live on after one has died. In time, however, those people also die and thus eventually the residue also fades and disappears. Even the most expansive terrestrial meaning will eventually vanish. It may take longer, but vanish it eventually will, if only because all humans will eventually become extinct.

This is not to deny that there are situations when death does enhance terrestrial meaning, at least in some ways. These are situations in which somebody dies for a (noble) cause, perhaps with the condition that the cause could not have been (as well) served without the cost of the person's life. The slavery abolitionist and martyr John Brown seems to have had this assessment of his own subsequent death (by execution) when he said, "I am worth inconceivably more to hang than for any other purpose."[2] Soldiers who sacrifice their lives in order to save the lives of a greater number of their comrades might also be thought to give meaning to their lives by their deaths.[3]

Even in such cases, however, death is not a solution to the human predicament. The lives of those who die remain cosmically insignificant, and while some terrestrial meaning is gained, other such meaning is lost, because one cannot generate the meaning that one would have generated if one had continued living. Moreover, the reason why these deaths have the capacity to produce as much terrestrial meaning as they do is precisely because they come at a very high cost—the annihilation of the person who dies.

All things considered then, death is not deliverance from the human predicament, but a further feature of it.

Is death bad?

There is, however, an ancient philosophical challenge to the widespread view that death is bad. According to this challenge, first advanced by the Epicureans (and which I shall therefore call Epicurean arguments) but developed by subsequent philosophers, death is not bad *for the person who dies*. The italicized qualification is crucial because nobody disputes that a person's death can be bad for bereaved family, friends, or other living people (or animals) who suffer the loss of the departed person.

The Epicurean arguments do not claim that death, understood as "(the process of) dying," cannot be bad for the person who dies. Death in that sense can be awful—filled with suffering and indignity. This is especially so when dying is protracted, as it often is for those who succumb to such conditions as cancer and progressive paralysis. Instead, the claim is that death in the sense of "being dead" is not bad for the deceased.

Sometimes, the question whether death is *bad* for the person who dies is framed in terms of whether death is a *harm* to the person who dies. However, these two questions are not identical. Although some accounts of harm refer to badness or, more usually, the related notion of making somebody "worse off," the concepts of "harm" and "bad" are not identical. What constitutes harm is arguably even more contentious than what constitutes badness. Fortunately, it is not necessary to engage the more contested question whether death harms the person who dies. For death to be a feature of somebody's predicament, it would be sufficient that death is bad for that person. I shall focus on that question.

There are a number of arguments for the conclusion that death is not bad for the person who dies, but consider first what Epicurus himself had to say in support of this conclusion:

Become accustomed to the belief that death is nothing to us. For all good and evil consists in sensation, but death is deprivation of sensation. And therefore a right understanding that death is nothing to us makes the mortality of life enjoyable, not because it adds to it an infinite span of time, but because it takes away the craving for immortality. For there is nothing terrible in life for the man who has truly comprehended that there is nothing terrible in not living. So that the man speaks but idly who says that he fears death not because it will be painful when it comes, but because it is painful in anticipation. For that which gives no trouble when it comes, is but an empty pain in anticipation. So death, the most terrifying of ills, is nothing to us, since so long as we exist death is not with us; but when death comes, then we do not exist. It does not then concern either the living or the dead, since for the former it is not, and the latter are no more.[4]

In this passage, Epicurus is counseling a certain attitude to death, namely, the attitude of indifference. Later I shall return to the question what attitude we should have toward death. Of prior interest is the fact that Epicurus recommends indifference at least partially on the grounds that death is not bad for the one who dies. His argument for this conclusion has been interpreted in various ways.

Hedonism (and its discontents)

On one interpretation, his hedonistic assumption seems crucial. This is the assumption that "all good and evil consists in sensation"—or perhaps more generally in "feeling."[5] The assumption is that good feelings are the only things that are *intrinsically* good and bad feelings are the only things that are *intrinsically* bad. Here, intrinsic good and bad are to be distinguished from *instrumental* good and bad. Something is instrumentally good, for example, insofar as it leads to something else that is good. That good may be another instrumental good, but eventually the chain must end with something that is intrinsically good—good in itself.

Hedonists do not deny that something other than feelings can be instrumentally either good or bad. Thus, something that involves no feeling in itself may be judged good or bad depending on whether it leads to either positive or negative feelings. For example, exposure to carcinogens may involve no negative feeling at the time of exposure, but it can be judged to be instrumentally bad because it leads to negative feelings when the resultant cancer manifests itself.

On the assumption that death ends all feeling, an assumption I do accept and that (contrary to some possible view of an afterlife) I think we should accept, the dead cannot have any feelings. From this, combined with the hedonistic assumptions about intrinsic value, it follows that nothing can be intrinsically bad (or good) for the dead.

One common response to this component of the Epicurean argument is to dispute the hedonistic assumption and claim that feelings do not exhaust the list of what can be intrinsically good or bad. Consider the following example: Your spouse is unfaithful to you by having sex with somebody else. This is done without your ever learning of the infidelity. (We can imagine either that you are sufficiently naïve and gullible or that your spouse is superbly cunning in his or her deceptions.) Moreover, your spouse, who maintains the usual sexual relations with you, is meticulous in the use of barrier contraception with the extramarital partner in order to protect you from sexually transmitted diseases that might otherwise be acquired from the other party.

It seems to many people that your spouse's dalliances are bad for you even though they do not lead to any bad feelings in you. If that is so, then perhaps death can be bad for the person who dies even though it leads to no bad feelings. Some hedonists are tempted to respond that, in the case of your spouse's infidelity, you *could* find out and thus experience negative feelings (even if, in fact, you do not), whereas in the case of death, there is no way that you could ever experience negative feelings after death. Critics of hedonism reply in turn that we can construct examples of bad things that could not cause you any negative feelings. Perhaps you have been mortally wounded in war and while you lie conscious but dying on the battlefield, your spouse, thousands of kilometers away, is copulating with your best friend. There is no way that you can learn of this before you die. (Those with fertile imaginations who begin wondering about instantaneous telecommunications, text messaging, and the like should imagine the same case in the eighteenth century when communication was slow.)

It is possible, of course, for hedonists simply to bite the bullet (that has ripped through your body on that distant battlefield) and deny that your spouse's infidelity is bad for you if you never find out about it. That position does seem to have some odd implications. For example, consider a scenario in which you *do* find out about your spouse's unfaithfulness. What is the main complaint against your spouse? Is it (a) that your spouse was unfaithful, or (b) that your spouse was careless enough for you to find out? The former seems correct, but for the bullet-biting hedonist, what was really bad for you was not the infidelity but rather finding out about it. Infidelity plus better deception would not have been bad for you. Thomas Nagel makes a similar point. He says: "The natural view is that the discovery of betrayal makes us unhappy because it is bad to be betrayed—not that betrayal is bad because its discovery makes us unhappy."[6]

Thus, one response to the Epicurean argument is to deny that hedonism is the correct account of intrinsic value (or of wellbeing). One might instead think that broader conceptions of what is good or bad for somebody are more appropriate. In other words, perhaps negative feelings are not the only things that are intrinsically bad. Perhaps it is also intrinsically bad if one's desires or preferences (such as for spousal fidelity or continued life) are not satisfied, irrespective of whether the dissatisfaction of those preferences causes negative feelings. Alternatively or in addition, perhaps some things (such as being betrayed, deceived, or cheated) are bad for one irrespective of whether one has a preference concerning them and whether or not they cause bad feelings. If we were to accept a conception of intrinsic value that is not restricted to positive and negative feelings, then it might be thought, despite the cessation of feeling that death brings, that death could still be bad for the deceased person.

The deprivation account

There is another response to the Epicurean argument—one that is available *even* to those who accept the Epicureans' hedonism. According to this response, death is bad (for the being who dies) because it deprives that individual of the good that he or she would otherwise have had. This is the deprivation account of the badness of death, and it is compatible with different views about what has intrinsic value. For those who accept the hedonist view, what is bad about death is (obviously) not that it involves any intrinsically bad feelings, but instead that it deprives the person who dies of the future good feelings that he would otherwise have had if he had not died when he did.

For those who have more extensive views about what has intrinsic value, death can deprive one of other intrinsic goods. For example, desire- or preference-satisfaction views would count the fulfillment of desires or preferences as intrinsic goods.[7] On such a view, if one had a preference to complete one's magnum opus, death would deprive one of an intrinsic good—the fulfillment of that preference—if one died before its completion. Of course, this is but one example. There are many other preferences that death prevents from being fulfilled—including the preference not to die! Death deprives us of the fulfillment of these desires and preferences.

The completion of important projects might also count as objective goods according to (at least some) so-called objective list theories. Thus, death before the completion of an important project might count as a deprivation of an intrinsic good according to such theories too.

Whichever view one takes of wellbeing, death is bad, according to the deprivation account, because it deprives the person who dies of the good that further life would have contained. Sometimes, however, a longer life would either have contained no good or it would have contained so much bad that any good would have been outweighed. In such circumstances, the deprivation account implies that death is not bad—or at least not bad all things considered.

This is not an implausible implication of the deprivation account. It is possible for the quality of life, irrespective of which view of wellbeing one has, to be (or to become) so bad that death is better than continued life. It is a further question whether suicide or euthanasia is the appropriate response to such circumstances—and I consider the suicide question in chapter 7. All we need recognize now is that death does not always deprive us of net good and that the deprivation account's implication that death may actually be preferable in such circumstances does not appear to be a disadvantage of the account. It may even be an advantage.

Annihilation

However, while the deprivation account enjoys widespread support, we should not assume that there has to be only one reason why death is bad for the being who dies. It is entirely possible that death is bad for more than one reason. It could be that the badness of death is, at least sometimes, overdetermined.

One possibility we should consider is that death is bad in large part because it annihilates the being who dies. Death is bad not merely because it deprives one of the future good that one would otherwise have had, but also because it *obliterates* one. Put another way, we have an interest not only in the future goods we would have if we continued living, but also an interest in continued existence itself. Death can deprive us of the goods and also thwart the interest in continued existence.

This is not to say that the interest in continued existence is so powerful that it is always in one's overall interest to continue living. My suggestion is compatible with thinking—and, indeed, I do think—that in some circumstances it is less bad to die than to continue living. Instead, the suggestion is only that, in dying, one loses not only whatever good that would otherwise have been in one's future, but also one's continued existence, in which one has an independent interest.

Despite this clarification, some people will be skeptical of my suggestion. They will argue that annihilation of a being is *only* bad if that person is deprived of good that he would otherwise have had. At the very most, they may concede that even when death is not bad all things considered, it may sometimes still be *partly* bad, but that would be the case only if the death deprived the being of *some* good despite its future being bad all things considered.

That is certainly one way in which a death that is, on balance, preferable may nonetheless be bad in some way. However, my claim is more expansive than that. It is that there is a further explanation for why death is bad—and the further explanation is that one's annihilation is an independent bad.

It is, of course, hard to *prove* this, but there are a number of considerations that support it. Even if some of these fail to convince, the weight of the considerations together makes the position, at the very least, plausible. I shall spell out some of these considerations, but I shall also show that the annihilation account has helpful applications and implications that count in its favor.

First, more can be said to explain why annihilation is a bad independent of any deprivation. Death brings a complete and irreversible end to the being from whose prudential perspective we are considering whether there is a deprivation. Annihilation of a being may not be the *worst* of fates for that being, but it certainly seems to involve a very significant loss—namely, loss of the self. Each individual, speaking in the first person, can say: "My death obliterates me. Not only am I deprived of future goods but *I* am also destroyed. This person, about whom I care so much, will cease to exist. My memories, values, beliefs, perspectives, hopes—my very self—will come to an end, and for all eternity." (This concern about annihilation of a person need not be restricted to that person. Other people can also recognize the badness of that annihilation.)

I am not inventing this worry. Annihilation seems to play an important part in people's concerns about death. If you ask people why they do not want to die, you will get that sort of answer at least as often as you will hear explanations about deprivation. People have very strong desires not to die, and death frustrates these desires.

Perhaps it will be suggested that this concern about the continued existence of the self is merely a deeply ingrained instinct with ancient evolutionary origins. Accordingly, it is pre-rational. The instinct—even though not the conscious rationalization of it—is no different from the least sophisticated life forms that also have a powerful self-preservation drive.

However, being *pre*-rational does not mean that it is *ir*rational.[8] Indeed, it seems strange that a prudential valuer would be concerned only about what he is deprived of and not also about the very existence of the being that would be deprived. To be a prudential valuer is to value things from the egoistic perspective. What's good or bad for oneself—the ego—is one kind of egoistic consideration, but the very continued existence of the ego is another good, and its annihilation is another bad.[9]

To say that the annihilation of the self or the ego is bad for the being that dies is not to commit to a metaphysically controversial view that there is some essential self that persists unaltered for the full duration of one's life. Instead, the relevant sense of self is entirely compatible with the view that what counts (prudentially) is not personal identity (in the strict, numerical sense of "identity"), but rather psychological continuity or connectedness.[10] After all, annihilation irrevocably terminates the string of psychologically connected states that constitute one's life, and that is something that a prudential valuer can regret.

Support for the badness of annihilation can also be drawn from Frances Kamm's "Limbo Man,"[11] who prefers "putting off a fixed quantity of goods of life by going into a coma and returning to consciousness at a later point to have them,"[12] rather than having those goods immediately and then dying. In other words, Limbo Man has a choice between two life options. Both contain the same amount of good, and thus the choice between the options is not a choice between lesser and greater deprivation. The choice is instead whether to live the life uninterrupted or to instead delay the later goods by entering the limbo of a coma. The advantage of the latter choice is to delay the point of annihilation.

Now a preference for such limbo would not be reasonable under all circumstances. If, for example, the coma lasted a very long time and one would awake, like Rip van Winkle, to find one's loved ones long deceased and be so utterly bewildered by the changed world that the goods one had delayed were now either impossible or eclipsed by the bad, then going into limbo might not be that attractive. However, we can simply stipulate that this is not the case. Perhaps one's loved ones similarly go into limbo and one can readily adapt to the new world. Limbo might also hold no special attraction if the post-limbo life is so brief that soon after emerging from limbo, one is annihilated. Again, we can stipulate that this is not the case—that the portion of life delayed is significant. Under such circumstances, many people might share Limbo Man's preference. Insofar as they do share the preference, this seems to be because they think that annihilation is a bad that one does best to delay.

Another, albeit much lesser, consideration in favor of taking annihilation to be part of the badness of death is that it is *consistent* with (but not the same as) judgments about the destruction of objects that lack prudential value but have value of another kind. If *damaging* an object of value is bad, then *annihilating* it—an extreme form of damage—is also bad. If damage to the Grand Canyon or the Mona Lisa, for example, would be bad, then their obliteration would also be bad.

This does not preclude the possibility that utterly destroying an item of value may be less bad, all things considered, than not doing so. Perhaps some art-hater has credibly threatened to burn down the entire Louvre unless the Mona Lisa is incinerated. It is also possible to think that it may sometimes be less bad to destroy an item of value than to damage it. (One possible explanation is that allowing it to persist in a damaged state would be a constant reminder of the loss of value, whereas its destruction would be a case of "out of sight, out of mind.") However, such thoughts do not undermine my point that destruction is a kind of damage and thus if damage is bad, destruction is also bad—even if destruction is the lesser of two bads. Even when annihilating something of value is the least bad of the options, it is nonetheless something to regret.

Paintings do not have prudential value, and many people—I am among them—deny that they have intrinsic moral value, but (some) paintings can have some kind of value. Something of value is lost when they are annihilated. It would be surprising if that were the case but that nothing of value were lost when a person is annihilated.[13]

The view that death is bad partly because of the annihilation it brings about is also supported by its implications. For example, it implies that even when one's future would have contained *no* good, death is nonetheless bad in an important way for the person who dies,[14] even though it is not bad all things considered. In such circumstances, death is the lesser of two evils rather than actually being not bad at all. This seems like the right implication for reasons I shall explain.

Some might find it hard to imagine a situation in which a death deprives somebody of *no* good. How difficult it is depends on what view of wellbeing one has. On a hedonistic view, it is actually remarkably easy to imagine such a situation. Consider a person with a terminal condition, who is so wracked by suffering that positive feelings are simply impossible. The negative experiences are so intense and overwhelming that positive experiences are unattainable. Imagine further that the only way to avoid these negative feelings, other than death, is to render the person insensate, in which case, positive experiences are impossible for another reason. In such cases, which are all too common, death (on the hedonistic view) deprives the being who dies of *no* intrinsic good.

Although it is common, in response to the death of such an unfortunate, to utter the platitude that his death was "a release," if we really believed that this was *all* it was (that there was *nothing* bad about the death for the person), then it seems it would be reasonable to celebrate rather than to mourn the death. It is true that those bereaved have suffered a loss. They must live the rest of their lives without ever being able to interact with their beloved deceased family member or friend again. It might be argued that it is the loss to the bereaved that we (and they) mourn. However, since meaningful interactions would have been impossible even if the person had not died, given how badly off he was, it is hard to see how the person's death would be a cause for mourning even for those bereaved—that is, unless the loss of the person himself counted for something.[15]

Those resistant to the idea that annihilation can be bad in itself for the one who dies might retort that we mourn the dead (for their sake) because it is only when they die that it becomes clear that there is no hope of better prospects—no hope that his condition will be reversed and that he will have positive value in his future.

This might explain some cases, but not others. There are situations in which the situation is clearly hopeless. Consider a person suffering from end-stage metastatic cancer or the final phases of a neurodegenerative disorder and whose end is imminent. Given the current state of medical knowledge and the present limits of the therapeutic arsenal, the chances of improvement, while not logically impossible, are actually so remote that hope is utterly and thoroughly misguided. It borders on hoping for imminent resurrection, in full health, of the recently deceased. Thus, the loss of hope cannot always explain why we should mourn those whose deaths deprived them of no good.

Perhaps what we are mourning after the death is the fact that the person became so badly ill that death deprived him of no good. However, mourning on that basis would also be implausibly timed. The peak of that mourning should have been while he was suffering and it became clear that death would deprive him of no good. *That* is when it was really bad. When the person who had been in that situation dies and is released from his suffering, the time for celebrating would have arrived—that is, unless the death, although preferable, nonetheless was a serious bad. That bad, I suggest, is the annihilation of the one who died. It is a bad feature of death even when death is the lesser of two evils. In other words, even when death is the least bad option, all things considered, there is still *something* lost.

Perhaps there is another explanation of our response to this case. Perhaps what we mourn is the loss of further consciousness.[16] If consciousness is viewed as a good independent of its contents, then even if the contents of consciousness are so appalling that it is less bad, all things considered, to lose consciousness permanently, the loss of consciousness may nonetheless be a bad and something to be mourned. This explanation is not at all implausible, but it is unclear how it differs from annihilation. The irreversible cessation of consciousness *is* annihilation of the conscious being. (Later I shall say more about different senses of "annihilation" and "death," and how, under some interpretations, death and annihilation do not always occur at the same time.)

There is a possible response to my arguments that death is bad not merely because of the goods of which it deprives the person who dies. This response is that the loss of the self is merely another deprivation brought about by death. According to this response, death can deprive one of various goods and among those is one's life itself. It would follow that the bad-ness of annihilation could be accounted for by the deprivation account alone.

Such a (re-)interpretation would render the deprivation account sympathetic to my claim that death is bad at least in part because it involves the annihilation of the being who dies. Thus, even when continued life would not have deprived the per-son who dies of any *other* goods, it would still be bad because it involved the annihilation of the being who dies. That is to say, death would still be an evil, albeit the lesser of two evils. My view is that death is an evil and thus part of the human predicament. It really makes no difference to that view whether we see the loss of one's life as the *deprivation* of an additional good or as a further loss over and above any deprivations it may cause. That further loss is the loss of the being who dies.

When is death bad for the person who dies?

As a response to the Epicurean argument, the deprivation account, even when augmented by the annihilation account, faces a number of difficulties. These difficulties also confront those who reject Epicurus's hedonistic assumptions. This is because Epicurus's argument has, at least on some interpreta-tions, a further feature—that in order for something to be bad for somebody, that being must actually exist (at the time at which the bad occurs). This claim, sometimes known as the "existence requirement"[17] may be read into Epicurus's statement that "death ... is nothing to us since so long as we exist death is not with us; but when death comes, then we do not exist."

The (implicit) suggestion is that unless one exists, one cannot be *deprived* of anything—whether positive feelings or non-experiential goods.[18] Nor, it is said, can anything bad—whether bad feelings or any fates that need not have any experiential component—befall one if one does not exist. In other words, to be deprived or to have something bad happen to one, one must actually exist. Things can be bad only for those who exist.

The existence requirement is denied by many (but not all) of those rejecting the Epicurean argument, including many of those who accept the deprivation account of death's badness. They deny that one must exist in order for something to be bad for one. More specifically, they deny that one must exist *at the time at which death is bad* for one who dies. The problem is that in denying this, they must grapple with the following question: *When* is death bad for the person who dies? Except in the case of death and of (purported) posthumous harms, we typically do not have difficulty stating the time at which the bad befalls the person for whom it is a bad.

Consider the case of Meg breaking her leg. The broken leg is bad for Meg from the time she breaks it until the time it is healed or, to be more accurate, until the time when any other effects of the injury have also vanished.[19] However, in the case of death (and posthumous harms), the answer to the timing question is not straightforward.

There have been a variety of answers to this question. Unsurprisingly, they all contain at least an element of truth. In some cases where they conflict, they seem to be responding to different interpretations of the question or picking out different elements of the time at which death is bad for the being who dies. Thus, it is worth sketching out the basic positions, their attractions, and common objections to them before attempting to formulate an overall view that draws on the insights of each.[20]

"Subsequentism": It seems natural—or at least *consistent* with the timing of other bad things—to say that death is bad *after* it happens. Just as the breaking of Meg's leg is bad for her after she breaks it, one might be tempted to say that Beth's death is bad for her after she dies. However, the purported difficulty with this view is that it requires us to accept that death is bad for Beth even though she no longer exists at the time at which it is said to be bad for her.

"Priorism": If it seems strange to say that death is bad for Beth at a time she no longer exists, one might be tempted to an alternative position, according to which death is bad for Beth *before* she dies.[21] However, that also seems strange, for how can something that happens later be bad for somebody who existed earlier? Some have suggested that this view commits one to a dubious metaphysical claim of "backward causation"—something earlier being caused by something later.

"Eternalism": A third alternative is that Beth's death is "eternally" bad for her (that is, bad for her at all times).[22] The suggestion here is that "when we say that her death is bad for her, we are really expressing a complex fact about the relative values of two possible lives"—one where she dies when she does and one in which she dies later—and "that if these possible lives stand in a certain value relation ... then they stand in that relation" not only when Beth exists but also when she does not.[23] In other words, it is always the case that it is bad for Beth that she will (or did) die at some point rather than living (or having lived) longer (on the assumption that the further life would have been worth living[24]). Some people find eternalism unsatisfactory because, though it tells us when it is *true* that Beth's death is bad for her, it does not tell us at which time death's badness befalls Beth.[25]

"Concurrentism": The answer to the latter question—when does death's badness befall Beth—seems to be "at the time when death occurs."[26] In this regard, death has something in common with other bad things that befall people. Although it may be eternally true that Meg's breaking her leg is bad for her, the time at which the badness befalls her is the time when she breaks her leg (even if the badness extends into the future). Similarly, the time at which the bad of Beth's death befalls her is the time when she dies.

"Atemporalism": Still others have suggested that it may be possible for good or bad to befall a person without it always being possible to temporally (or even spatially) locate all those goods and ills.[27] Thomas Nagel provides the example of an intelligent person who incurs "a brain injury that reduces him to the mental condition of a contented infant."[28] Even if that person were well cared for, he notes, we would regard this fate as a misfortune. Yet it is hard to say exactly when the misfortune befalls him. The intelligent person, he says, no longer exists after the brain injury, and the person with the mental condition of a contented infant does not exist before it. This, says Thomas Nagel, "should convince us that it is arbitrary to restrict the goods and evils that can befall a man to nonrelational properties ascribable to him at particular times."[29]

These responses are all interesting, and perhaps one of them is correct. However, I want to consider a response that draws on insights from a few of these responses. In attempting to determine the time at which death is bad for the person who dies, it is helpful to begin with a case in which, according to the Epicureans, there is no special difficulty in stating the time at which something bad befalls somebody. Consider the case of Meg breaking her leg. Of this case, we can say the following:

a. Meg is the person for whom the broken leg is bad.
b. The period during which her leg is broken and in which any resultant (psychological or other) negative effects persist is the time during which the broken leg is bad for Meg.
c. That period begins with the breaking of the leg, and thus that is the time when the bad first befalls her, even though the badness of the broken leg is clearly not restricted to that instant (and may even not be felt in that moment if, for example, she is unconscious at the time).
d. According to at least some views,[30] it is always (or "eternally") true—before Meg breaks her leg, while it is broken, and after it has healed—that Meg's breaking her leg is bad for her during the period in which her leg is broken.[31]

These points are depicted visually in figure 5.1.

Epicureans think that we can identify the time during which the broken leg is bad for Meg because that badness exists while Meg exists. If we turn from Meg's leg to Beth's death, we find that the latter cannot be exactly like the former because death has a unique feature. It ends somebody's existence. The being whom the bad befalls ceases to exist. We must expect that this difference will require us to analyze the badness of death *somewhat* differently.

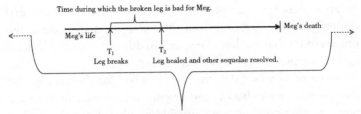

Time at which it is true that between T_1 and T_2 the broken leg was bad for Meg.

FIGURE 5.1 Meg's broken leg.

More specifically, to insist on the existence requirement—namely, the requirement that in order for something to be bad for somebody, that person must exist at the time it is bad for him—is either to preclude the possibility that death can be bad or to require some contortion (arguably such as priorism) to ensure that death meets the requirement.

However, I see no reason why we should treat the existence requirement *as* a requirement. To insist that the badness of death must be analyzed in exactly the same way as other bad things that do not have the distinctive feature of death is to be insensitive to a complexity in the way the world is. It is a procrustean insistence that relevant differences must be eliminated to ensure conceptual conformity. In other words, we face the following choices:

1. Recognize that death is different from other bad things;

or

2. Insist that despite the differences, unless death can fit, in every respect, our usual analysis of when it is bad, it is, contrary to appearances, not actually bad.

"Clever" people[32] may prefer the second option, but the first option is, I believe, the wise one. It is wise for many reasons, but one reason is that we should respond to difference with difference and to complexity with nuance.

Those of us who think that death is bad for the person who dies do not have to bow to the Epicurean insistence on the existence requirement. We can provide another account of when death is bad for the person who dies—one that does not presuppose the existence requirement. Paralleling the claims that were made about Meg, we can say the following about Beth:

a. Beth is the person for whom the death is bad.
b. The period during which Beth is dead is the period during which her death is bad for her.
c. That period begins with the moment of Beth's death and thus that is the time when the bad first befalls her, even though the badness of death is clearly not restricted to that instant (and will not be felt, as death terminates consciousness).
d. According to at least some views, it is always (or "eternally") true—both while Beth is alive and after she is dead—that her death is bad for her during the period when she is dead.

For a visual depiction of these claims, see figure 5.2.

This collection of claims has elements of the different views, outlined earlier, about when death is bad for the one who dies. It identifies the ante-mortem Beth as the being that the bad befalls. In this regard, it has *something* in common with priorism. However, unlike priorism, which attempts to meet the existence requirement by having the bad and the victim of that bad coexist, my view says that the bad of death befalls somebody when it

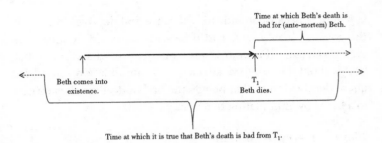

FIGURE 5.2 Beth's death.

first occurs and that it continues to be bad for as long as it lasts. This is consistent with our timing of other bads and includes elements of both concurrentism and subsequentism. Like concurrentism, it recognizes that the bad of death first befalls somebody the moment that being dies. That is the point at which the person is annihilated and deprived of all future goods that she would otherwise have had. However, the annihilation and deprivation do not exist for a mere moment. They endure for the remainder of eternity, for that is what it is to be annihilated and deprived of *all* future good. In this regard, my view recognizes a truth in subsequentism. My view also acknowledges the insight of eternalism by recognizing that (at least according to some views) it is always true, even before Beth dies, that the later fact of her death is bad for her.

In other words, my view parallels ordinary cases of bad in all respects except one. The one respect in which it differs is the one respect in which death[33] differs from ordinary bads. It denies that a person must exist at the time he is dead in order for death to be bad for that person. The reason why death is bad for that person is precisely because it ends his existence and deprives him of all the good he would have had if he had continued existing. The view involves no "backward causation" because whatever it is that brings about the being's death causes the annihilation and subsequent deprivation of that being. The bad of death is thus caused to a being by annihilating that being.

The symmetry argument

There is a further Epicurean argument for the conclusion that death is not bad for the one who dies. This argument, credited to Lucretius, begins with the observation that we do not regret the period of our nonexistence before we were born. From this it is inferred that we should have a similar attitude to the period of nonexistence that follows our death.

We should not take too literally the reference to our birth because there is good reason to think that we come into existence before we emerge from the womb, the time usually referred to as one's birth. Thus, following Frederik Kaufman, I shall speak instead of "pre-vital nonexistence" and will contrast this, as he does, with "post-mortem nonexistence."[34]

Lucretius's argument, like Epicurus's before him, is about our attitude toward death. However, we can construe the argument in such a way that it speaks to the question whether death is bad. So construed, the argument claims that because our pre-vital nonexistence was not bad, neither is our postmortem nonexistence.

This argument assumes that one's pre-vital nonexistence and one's postmortem nonexistence are evaluatively symmetrical. One possible response to Lucretius, other than simply endorsing his argument, is to accept the symmetry he assumes, but to argue that the mistaken evaluation is not the one about death but instead the one about pre-vital nonexistence. According to this view, pre-vital nonexistence is bad for the one who subsequently comes into existence. If the two periods of nonexistence are symmetrical, then one can continue to claim that postmortem nonexistence is also bad.

That response is highly implausible. Lucretius is entirely correct in taking pre-vital existence not to be bad. His mistake lies in his assumption of evaluative symmetry between the two periods of nonexistence. There are crucial differences between these two periods that should lead us to think that only postmortem nonexistence is bad.

The relevant difference is not the fact that (at least with regard to bad things) we have a deep-seated bias toward the future[35]—that we are far more concerned about bad that will still befall us than we are about bad that has already befallen us. This is not the relevant difference because it is entirely possible that although we have this psychological bias, a bad is no worse merely because it is in the future rather than in the past. To show that future nonexistence is bad even though past nonexistence is not, we need to point to something other than our attitudes to these two periods of nonexistence. We need to show why postmortem nonexistence is actually bad even though pre-vital nonexistence is not.

The purported problem with attempting to do this is that the deprivation account seems to imply that pre-vital nonexistence *is* bad because it deprives one of the good that one would have had if one had come into existence earlier. This assumes, of course, that one would have lived longer (or had a better life) if one had come into existence earlier. If the same lifespan had simply shifted earlier in time, then one's actual later birth would not have deprived one of good that one would not otherwise have had,[36] unless one's earlier birth would have resulted in one living in a time in which one's life would have been better.

One important response to this problem is that while death does deprive the one who dies, pre-vital nonexistence involves no deprivation. To this end, Frederik Kaufman helpfully distinguishes between "thin" and "thick" interpretations of what it is to be a particular person. On a thin interpretation, a person is some metaphysical essence, whether that is "a certain human body, a particular genetic construction, a certain origin, the brain, a Cartesian soul, or whatever."[37] If we take this view of a person, then it may be possible, he says, to think of somebody having come into existence much earlier than he did and thus to be deprived of the goods between that earlier possible start and the time he actually came into existence.

However, when somebody is concerned about his death, he is typically concerned about the end of his "conscious personal existence"[38] (that is, about the end of the being with his memories, consciousness, attachments, values, beliefs, desires, goals, and perspectives). Thus, the concern is about the end of a person understood in this thick way.

We know that the concern about death is a concern about the end of persons in the thick rather than the thin sense because fates, such as a permanent coma, that preserve the metaphysical essence of the person but bring an end of the person in the richer, thicker, biographical sense of "person" are disturbing for the same kinds of reasons that death is disturbing.[39] For example, they deprive one of the goods that one would otherwise have had.

A person understood in the thick way could not have come into existence *significantly* earlier than he did. The claim is not that a person could not have come into existence *somewhat* earlier than he did. Imagine a person who was created from a particular sperm and ovum that were harvested and then frozen for a while before in vitro fertilization took place. In such a case, there could have been some variation in the time at which the person came into existence. However, even in such cases, if the fertilization had been much earlier, a different person, in the thick sense, would have resulted. Given that our biographical personhood is a product of, among other things, who raised us, what their circumstances were when they raised us, what interests and views we had, and what we did, each of us could not have come into existence much earlier (or later) than we did.

Now, if one could not have come into existence much earlier than one did in fact come into existence, then one could not have been (significantly) deprived by one's pre-vital nonexistence. This is asymmetrical with the end of life. Once a person, in the thick, biographical sense, already exists, the biography could have continued had the person not died when he did. Death can thus deprive the person who dies.

It is true, of course, that if a person lived *much* longer than he in fact lived, then there might be significant changes in personality—changes so marked that it might be argued that the later person was, in the biographical sense, different from the earlier one. That is actually one reason why some people think that while death can deprive and is thus bad, it would not be good to live forever. The idea is that while death is bad, its badness would eventually run out. I shall consider this argument in the next chapter, when I discuss whether immortality would be good. For now, we need only note that one would have to live for a *really* long time for this purported problem to arrive. Extending one's life by a significant period is unlikely to lead to psychological changes that are any more marked than those that already occur within an ordinary human lifespan. At the very least, the death deprives us of good that pre-vital nonexistence does not. They are thus different, and the Lucretian assumption of symmetry is mistaken.

There is a further way in which pre-vital and postmortem nonexistence are not symmetrical. Death, as I argued earlier, is bad not merely because it deprives, but also because it annihilates. Pre-vital nonexistence does not—and could not possibly—annihilate. None of us has an interest in coming into existence. If we had never come into existence, no interest would have been thwarted. (I have gone so far as to argue— although I shall not repeat the argument here—that it is actually better never to come into existence.[40]) However, once we do exist, we acquire and then have an interest in continuing to exist. This interest can be defeated by other interests—such as interests in being spared fates worse than death. However, once one exists, there is at least *an* interest in continued existence that death thwarts.[41]

To say that, once one comes into existence, one has an interest in continued existence requires some qualification. There are different senses in which one comes into existence. One comes into existence as a biological organism at a different time from when one comes into existence as a sentient being, for example. To say that, once one comes into existence, one has an interest in continuing to exist leaves open the question which sense of "coming into existence" is the relevant one. In other words, it does not answer the question about when one acquires the interest in continuing to exist. That question does not need to be settled in order to accept the point that death thwarts an interest of those who have come into existence in the relevant sense (whatever the relevant sense may be).[42]

Some may wonder how two of my views can be reconciled: How can it be better never to have come into existence but also be a bad to cease to exist? One reason it is better never to come into existence is that one does not face annihilation. Never existing does not carry that cost, but ceasing to exist does. Existence also carries innumerable other costs. These include various assaults on the quality of life (discussed in chapter 4), as well as the absence of meaningfulness to varying degrees (discussed in chapter 3). There is invulnerability to all of those if one never exists. By coming into existence, many of these costs are inescapable, and one becomes vulnerable to others. This is why it is better never to come into existence. Death is a release from only some of these existential burdens. Thus, while it returns us to a state of immunity to some fates—such as physical or mental suffering—it does so at considerable cost. It can deprive us of some goods. It also thwarts the interest we have in continuing to exist. It obliterates us.

Taking Epicureans seriously?

There are good reasons for rejecting the Epicurean view that death is not bad for the one who dies. However, one cannot claim that the Epicurean position has been decisively refuted. It has remained a remarkably resilient challenge to the widespread view that death is bad for us. There have been and there still are some philosophers who think that the best arguments support rather than undermine the Epicurean view. That they are in the minority does not mean that they are wrong.

As a practical matter, we have to reach some view about whether death is bad—even if it is a tentative or working view that we might in principle revise should better arguments come to light. Agnosticism on the question may be acceptable in some situations, but there are many others in which we have to make a decision one way or the other.

To this end, it helps to consider what would be involved in accepting the Epicurean view. First, we would have to revise our views about how bad *painless* murder is. It is true that such murder would have effects on those who continue to live after the death of the murder "victim." (The scare quotes become necessary if we are Epicureans because one cannot be a victim if nothing bad has happened to one.) However, it is hard to justify taking murder quite as seriously as we do if its badness consists only in what it does to those who are left behind. Consider a case of abduction, in which those who miss the abductee do not know (for the remainder of their lives) whether she is alive or dead. Such an abduction would presumably be worse than murder, for abduction would be bad for the abductee *and* those who miss her, whereas murder would be bad only for those who miss the "victim."

Perhaps it will be suggested that (painless) murder would remain one of the most serious crimes because of the fear it instills in people. The Epicurean would view that fear as irrational, but perhaps the suggestion is that social policy should take even irrational fears into account. However, that would open the way to justifying harsher penalties for "black" rapists of "white" victims in (majority "white") racist societies in which there were irrationally greater fears of "black-on-white" rape.

This is not to say that the effects on the living would not be sufficient to retain the serious crime status for murder. It is only to say that painless murder would have to be viewed as a less serious crime than it currently is.

For those who are not convinced by that argument, consider the following scenario:

A terrorist has an Epicurean tied down. He forces a gun into the Epicurean's mouth and keeps threatening to pull the trigger. If the threat is acted upon, it will kill the Epicurean instantly. Either (a) the Epicurean remains true to his belief that "death is nothing to us" and sits there unperturbed, or (b) he is unable to conform his emotions to his beliefs and is filled with anxiety, perhaps to the extent that he soils himself.

In (a), the Epicurean is committed to thinking that it makes no difference to him whether the attempted terrorizing is followed by the pulling of the trigger. The death would not be bad for the Epicurean. Although it might be bad for the Epicurean's loved ones, because the Epicurean will be dead, the impact of his death on his family should make no difference to him either. In (b), the Epicurean is committed to thinking that it would be bad for him if the terrorist did *not* pull the trigger, because if he is not killed, he will suffer all kinds of post-traumatic stress.

Curiously, though, this does not imply—for the Epicurean—that pulling the trigger would be *good*, even though the earlier that he is killed, the less of the terrorizing he will have to endure. Just as Epicureans cannot think that death is bad, so they cannot think that death is good (or even less bad). If death cannot be bad because one no longer exists and can no longer experience anything, then for the same reasons, death cannot be good.

This applies not merely to the hypothetical case of the terrorized Epicurean, but also to innumerable cases in which people are suffering unspeakably at the end of their lives. In such cases, the Epicurean cannot say that death would be good (or even less bad) for the person who is suffering.[43] In other words, even when the quality of life has become so bad that life has ceased to be worth continuing, the Epicurean is unable to say that death is less bad than continued life.

These are very big bullets for the Epicurean to bite (at point-blank range). There are people who *say* that they accept these implications. We could put them to the test, but it would be unethical to do so (at least if I am right).

There is a further consideration. There are not definitive, watertight arguments against committed sceptics about, for example, the existence of the external world or about causation. These sceptics raise interesting philosophical issues that are certainly worth thinking about and discussing, but that does not mean that we should believe and act as if there were no external world or no causation. Arguments that death is not bad seem to be of the same kind. They are fine for the seminar room, but one seems to have lost perspective if one genuinely accepts the conclusion—if one thinks, for example, that killing somebody (painlessly) is never bad for that person.

We have very strong prima facie reasons for thinking that death is bad for the person who dies—and some powerful arguments to support this. If we encounter an argument that suggests otherwise, we have more reason to think that we are dealing with a philosophical puzzle to which we cannot find a definitive solution than that the argument actually establishes the conclusion.

Some might argue that we should have precisely the same reaction to any argument that yields the conclusion that it is better never to come into existence. However, there are massive differences between an argument that coming into existence is bad and an argument that death is not bad. First, the conclusion that death is never bad for the one who dies requires major upheaval in our moral views, as I have noted. By contrast, the conclusion that coming into existence is (very) bad, although disruptive of ordinary views about procreation, is actually entirely congruent with our other views about what is bad. We think it is bad to endure pain, suffering, frustration, sadness, trauma, to be betrayed, discredited, and to die. Coming into existence is the enabling condition for all these bad things and the guarantor of many of them.[44] Thus, the view that it is bad to be (vulnerable to such fates) is actually not at all surprising.

Second, if, on the strength of the Epicurean argument, we were to kill people painlessly and it turned out that the Epicureans were mistaken, there would have been massive moral costs attached to that error. We would have inflicted something seriously bad on those we had killed. By contrast, if we acted on the anti-natalist view and failed to bring people into existence, and it then turned out that the anti-natalist was mistaken, we would not have inflicted anything bad on anybody by failing to bring them into existence.

Thus, while there remain some defenders of the Epicurean view, and while we should continue to engage their arguments, it seems unreasonable to deny that death is part of the human predicament merely because we cannot offer so decisive an argument that the Epicurean position no longer holds any appeal for any philosopher.

How bad are different deaths?

Among those who agree that death is bad, there is disagreement about how bad it is in different circumstances. For example, if one thinks that the deprivation account is an exhaustive account of the badness of death, then one will tend to think that the younger one is when one dies, the worse death is. This is because, all things being equal, the earlier one dies, the more future good there is of which death deprives one. All things are not equal when one's future runs out of sufficient good earlier in one's life, in which case, an earlier death would be less bad (or not bad at all). However, in most cases, it is worse to die when one is young than when one is old.

This seems to be in accord with widely held views that "premature" deaths—deaths of young people—are especially tragic. This seems plausible, at least to some extent. However, the deprivation account as an exhaustive account of the badness of death implies that the *worst* time to die is immediately after one comes into existence. Thus, it is worse to die just after one comes into existence than when one is ten or twenty years old, for example.

Some are prepared to embrace this implication. However, when the implication is scrutinized more closely, it becomes implausible. As I indicated before, the point at which one comes into existence depends on what sense of coming into existence one has in mind. If one thinks that one comes into existence, in the relevant sense, at conception, then the worst time to die according to the (un-augmented) deprivation account is immediately after conception. Dying then would be much worse than dying when one was twenty. That is difficult to believe.

It is more plausible to think that one comes into existence in the relevant sense when one becomes sentient (which is late in gestation[45]). However, combining even that view with the un-augmented deprivation account leads to the conclusion that death in infancy is worse than death at twenty. This is only some-what less implausible than the claim that death immediately after conception is worse than death at twenty.

Implications such as these have led Jeff McMahan to think that the deprivation account needs to be supplemented (rather than replaced) with what he calls the "time-relative interest account" of death's badness.[46] According to this account, the badness of death must be "based on the effect that the death has on the vic-tim as he is at the time of death rather than on the effect it has on his life as a whole."[47] In other words, we must not compare how much good there would have been in a life if it ended in infancy with how much good there would have been in that life if it had ended at age twenty. Instead, we must ask how much the death deprives the being, relative to the interests of the being at the time of death.

It may be unclear what that means, and thus some expla-nation may help. Infants (and a fortiori zygotes) have very little (or, in the case of zygotes, no) psychological connection with those beings into which they would have developed and whom death deprives of good. Accordingly, if they die, they are deprived of less because they have less interest in the goods of which death deprives them. More generally, in determining the badness of death, we must discount the deprivation to the extent that there is not psychological unity between the being at the time he dies and the later being into which he would have developed.

The implication of this is that death at the early stages of existence is less bad than it is later. It becomes worse as the psychological properties of a person develop, because these properties create psychological unity with the future self whom death deprives of various goods. Then, as one ages beyond one's prime, the badness of death gradually diminishes, not because of a lack of psychological unity, but rather because death deprives one of less.

The annihilation account of death's badness may not seem, on the face of it, to address the problem that the time-relative interest account does. Indeed, it may appear to require the same corrective as the (un-augmented) deprivation account. If it is thought that annihilation is bad, then one might think that, all else being equal, it is worse to be annihilated earlier rather than later. That in turn might be thought to imply that annihilation immediately after coming into existence, as the earliest possible annihilation, is the worst. However, once we recall why annihilation is bad, we see that it actually produces a similar result to the time-relative interest account, at least with regard to the earliest stages of life.[48]

Annihilation, I said earlier, thwarts an interest in continued existence that one acquires when one comes into existence. However, when does one come into existence? The answer depends on what kind of existence is relevant. The human organism arguably comes into existence at conception or soon thereafter. However, that does not seem to be the sort of existence that we have an interest in continuing. If it were, then being reduced to a permanent vegetative state would not thwart our interest in continued existence, yet being reduced to such a state seems indistinguishable from death from a prudential perspective.

One's self or ego is as annihilated by the onset of a permanent vegetative state as it is by death. In both cases, the prudential valuer is obliterated.

The kind of existence we have an interest in continuing is existence as a person. This in turn requires sentience and sapience, both of which emerge slowly and in degrees after the human organism has already come into existence. Thus, coming into existence as a person is a process. At least two conclusions can be drawn from this. First, because there is no precise time at which one comes into existence as a person, there is no time "*immediately* after coming into existence" as a person (just as there is no time "*immediately* after becoming bald," given that becoming bald is also a process).

Second, and more importantly, we should fully expect that the interest in *continuing* to exist emerges gradually as one comes into existence as a person. If that is the case, however, why should we think that those still acquiring the psychological attributes required for the kind of life that we have an interest in continuing have as strong an interest in continued existence as those who already have all those attributes?

This is not to say that the death of merely sentient beings is not bad. I happen to think that it is bad (although I shall not argue for that here). Instead, my point is that, as bad as the death of a late-term fetus or an infant is, the death of an older child or young adult is still worse.

The deprivation account faces another difficulty in explaining how bad death is—a difficulty that the time-relative interest account cannot solve. This is what has become known as the problem of overdetermination[49] because it arises in cases where somebody's death in the near future is overdetermined. If he does not die of one cause, he will die of another. Jeff McMahan provides the following example:

> *The Cavalry Officer.* A gallant young cavalry officer is shot and killed during the charge of the Light Brigade by a Russian soldier named Ivan. If he had not been killed by Ivan, however, he would have been killed only seconds later by a bullet fired by another soldier, Boris, who also had him in his sights.[50]

The challenge to the deprivation account is that it seems that the officer's death is not very bad for him because his death at that moment deprived him of only a few seconds of life. (Given that those few seconds were probably not good seconds, Ivan's killing him may actually have deprived the officer of *nothing* good, making his death not bad at all.)

Fred Feldman has responded that the relevant counterfactual in determining the badness of the officer's death is not his death seconds later, but rather his not dying in his youth.[51] Jeff McMahan argues that this response is unsatisfactory. First, instead of assessing a *particular* death (death by Ivan's bullet), it assesses a *type* of death (death in the near future).[52] Second, it is arbitrary to characterize the officer's misfortune as "dying young" as there is no reason why we should not instead characterize the misfortune as dying "prematurely" or "before reaching old age" or "before attaining the maximum human lifespan" or even dying at all.[53]

The annihilation account can help here. The officer's death—his particular death from Ivan's bullet—is very bad even if it deprives him of only seconds of (good) life. It is bad because it annihilates him. The fact that he would have been killed by Boris if he had not been killed by Ivan may mean that his death from Ivan's bullet deprived him of very little if anything. However, Ivan's bullet annihilated him, and the badness of that is not limited by the fact that if Ivan had not killed him, then he would have suffered the same bad—annihilation—as a result of Boris shooting him. The timing of annihilation is not what makes it bad. The annihilation itself is bad. Thus, whether the officer is killed by Ivan or by Boris, or dies "prematurely" or "before reaching old age" or "before attaining the maximum human lifespan" or indeed, at any time,[54] he has been annihilated—and that is bad.

This does not mean that once one has fully come into existence in the relevant sense, one should be indifferent between varying times at which one might be annihilated. This is true even if we put aside concerns about how the timing of one's annihilation might affect the extent to which one is deprived. Annihilation is the sort of misfortune that, absent any overriding consideration, is best delayed as long as possible.[55] This is because it is not the sort of misfortune that one can "get over,"[56] for the obvious reason that (unlike diamonds, which are only for a very long time) death really is *forever*.

More needs to be said about death later in life. The outer limits of human longevity are currently around 120 years, but only a miniscule proportion of people reach such an age. The number of centenarians is increasing, but living into one's nineties is currently regarded as a long life. Many are inclined to offer purportedly comforting but blasé utterances about deaths at such advanced ages. For example, it is said of those who die at such an age that they had a "good innings." It is as if the subject matter were a cricket match rather than the annihilation of a person.

Perhaps an un-augmented deprivation view underlies such comments. Those who have had a good innings cannot expect to live much longer, given the (current) limits of human longevity, and thus their deaths do not deprive them of much that is good. That does assume that we should take the current limits of human longevity as the benchmark, but given the current facts about the world, that may not be an unreasonable assumption, regrettable though the facts may be.

Adding the annihilation view to the deprivation account leads to a less sanguine view about death in old age. No matter how good an innings one has had, death is a bad. It may be worse to be annihilated earlier (and not only because one is deprived of more), but it is still very bad to be annihilated later (even though one is deprived of less). Even a death at the very limit of human longevity is a bad. Again, it may not be bad all things considered, but it has a seriously bad feature.

Both the terms "death" and "annihilation" are ambiguous. Explicating that ambiguity reveals why some might think that death is not always a bad according to the annihilation account. Under some interpretations and applied to some entities, both terms have the same meaning. The annihilation of a person is the death of that person. However, there are other interpretations such that annihilation can occur in the absence of death.[57] Diseases such as dementia or conditions such as permanent vegetative states can annihilate one (in a psychological sense) before one dies (in a biological sense). If one distinguishes annihilation from death in this way, then there are some cases where (biological) death does not annihilate. This is because the person was annihilated before death, by the dementia or the permanent vegetative state. In these cases, death is not bad according to the annihilation account. However, that is only because the person was *already* annihilated by what came before (biological) death. Whatever it was that annihilated the person before death is what is then bad according to the annihilation view.[58]

Those who prefer not to distinguish death from annihilation can also account for such cases. They can say that psychological annihilation is psychological death and that it is psychological death that is fundamentally bad. Biological death is bad only insofar as it causes psychological death.

Living in the shadow of death

Epicurus and Lucretius argue that one should have an attitude of indifference to one's own death. They were responding to the many people who have (often intensely) negative attitudes toward death. Among these negative attitudes are terror, fear, dread, sadness, and anxiety. But we should distinguish the question whether death is bad from questions about our attitudes toward death.

Nor is there only one question about our attitudes toward death. First, there are psychological questions about what attitudes people *do* have and why they have them. Most, but not all, people have a negative attitude toward death. The precise attitude, as well as its intensity, may vary. This variation exists between people. Some are more averse to death than others. However, the variation may also exist within a person, who may have different attitudes at different times. Sometimes, the variation within a person depends on the moment, and sometimes, it depends on the stage of life. Somebody who fears death in youth may eagerly await it while suffering the final stages of a terminal condition. Alternatively, somebody who is indifferent while young may come to dread it as his remaining life expectancy reduces and the prospect of death becomes more vivid.

Second, there are questions about what attitudes toward death are *appropriate*. Merely because people have certain attitudes does not mean that those attitudes are always appropriate. Indeed, that is the Epicurean view—that the widespread fear of death is inappropriate. I have rejected the Epicurean basis for claiming that negative attitudes to death are unwarranted. There are, however, some spurious grounds for negative attitudes towards death. If, for example, somebody fears death because they will (experientially) miss those who survive them, then the attitude is inappropriate if death is, as I have assumed, extinction. The deceased may miss *out* on (that is, be deprived of) further experiences of those who survive them, and they may be missed by those who survive them, but they will not have the experience of missing anybody. Similarly, the atheist T-shirt that reads "Smile: There is no hell"[59] suggests that fearing death because one believes that one will roast in hell is inappropriate.

I have argued that death is bad. Sometimes, the badness of death is overdetermined. That is to say, it is bad both because it deprives us of further goods and because it annihilates us. In other circumstances, death may deprive one of no good. Then it is bad only because it annihilates us. If death is bad, then negative attitudes toward it are appropriate.

It is a further question to ask *which* negative attitudes are appropriate. Some people have taken issue with particular attitudes, arguing, for example, that fear is unwarranted because fear is appropriate only when what is feared is not a certainty.[60] I am not convinced by this claim. It seems entirely reasonable to fear some terrible fate, certain though it may be. However, if one wants either to impose that appropriateness condition on fear or to stipulate a definition of fear that implies such a condition, one can still think that other negative attitudes are appropriate. If "terror" does not connote an extreme form of fear, then that would be one possibility. Another would be "dread," although it is not clear to me how we can differentiate between fear and dread, short of stipulating differences.

The point is that it is appropriate to have some serious negative attitude in response to something that is seriously bad. If one's semantic quibbles exclude all the standard words we would use to describe the sort of attitudinal response that is reasonable, then one should suspect that the pedantry is inspired by unbridled optimism. If we have no word that the optimistic pedant thinks appropriate, we should just invent one. The crucial question is not a linguistic one, but rather whether it is reasonable to have a negative attitude to something bad. Self-imposed linguistic limits should not stand in the way of naming that attitude.

What attitude toward death is appropriate need not be invariant. It may be entirely appropriate for a person facing unbearable suffering to welcome death, all things considered, even while deeply regretting that annihilation is the only means to avoiding this fate worse than death. Whereas ambivalence about death might be appropriate for this person, it may be inappropriate for somebody who has much to lose by going the way of the dodo. In other words, an appropriate attitude in some circumstances may be an inappropriate attitude in others.

In addition to asking what attitudes toward death are appropriate, we might ask what attitude we *ought* to have. Some might think that we ought to have those (and only those) attitudes that are appropriate. However, it is possible for an attitude toward death to be appropriate and yet be an attitude that one ought not to have. For example, it might be entirely appropriate to be deeply depressed about the appalling fact that one is going to die, and yet there might be strong, prudential reasons not to become this morose. One might simply make one's life worse by adopting an appropriate attitude.

Perhaps it will be argued in response that any attitude that made one's life worse would not be an appropriate attitude. However, it is hard to see how that can be true unless one conflates "appropriate response" with "a response that one ought to have." It is appropriate to respond to bad things with a negative attitude and to terrible things with *very* negative attitudes. Yet it may be wise to temper an entirely appropriate negative attitude. For example, if one is seriously wronged, it is apposite to feel deeply aggrieved. If the wrong is not rectified, it is utterly fitting to continue to feel that way. The feeling is not misplaced. However, if feeling that way only perpetuates one's victimhood and makes one's life worse, there may be good reason to moderate one's appropriate feelings despite the fact that the wrong has not been repaired and the wrongdoer has not repented.

Dwelling on the facts of death can certainly make life miserable. Most people find ways of coping. I shall discuss some unduly optimistic coping mechanisms in the next chapter (on immortality). These include denial, fantasies about immortality, and sour grapes in response to the impossibility of immortality.

A more realistic and reasonable response is to retain a keen awareness of death's shadow but not to dwell on it all the time. One presses on with one's life, doing what one can to enhance its quality and meaning. Because meaning involves transcending one's own limits, such an enterprise may—if it has meaning worth pursuing—also involve enhancing the quality and sometimes the meaning of others' lives.

This is not denial because it is consistent with having existentially reflective moments in which one fully acknowledges the horror of death. There may be *many* such moments for those who are especially sensitive to (this feature of) the human predicament. Sometimes, these moments will be triggered by external stimuli such as deaths of others or threats to life. On other occasions, the thoughts will arise from (sometimes unconscious) stimuli within. Confronting and acknowledging the tragedy of death is why it is not the denial of death.

Coping with the prospect of death is easier the less imminently it looms. Of course, any one of us could die at any time. A lurking aneurysm may burst, a tsunami may engulf, bullets and other projectiles may pierce vital organs, or falling objects may crush. Those are the surprise attacks. When it threatens more openly, it is harder to ignore and harder to manage.

There is a tendency to admire those who manage to retain their composure in such circumstances and stare death in the face. This tendency may be explained in part by an implicit acknowledgment of just how difficult that is. However, it is difficult to escape the thought that praise of such stoicism is also aimed at discouraging those who cannot face death the way we like to see it faced—namely, "bravely." Seeing people fall apart in the face of their imminent death, or the threat thereof, only highlights our own mortality and makes us extremely uncomfortable.

There is a generational march from womb to grave. The oldest people are at the front. In the least bad circumstances, the Grim Reaper first cuts them down with his bloodied scythe. Their place is taken by the next generation and then by the next. One's grand-parents die, and soon one's parents have limited remaining life expectancy. Before long, one finds oneself in the front line staring death in the face.

The least bad circumstances are often not the actual circum-stances. Those in the younger ranks are often victims of the Grim Reaper's snipers who pick out targets among those whose "turn" we feel should not yet have arrived. One of many places where we see glaring evidence of the inequalities in age at death is in the obituary headlines in such newspapers as the *New York Times*. Here one reads, for example, that "Benzion Netanyahu, Hawkish Scholar, Dies at 102,"[61] "Albert O. Hirschman, Economist and Resistance Figure, Dies at 97," "Carolyn Rovee-Collier, Who Said Babies Have Clear Memories, Is Dead at 72," "Terry Pratchett, Novelist, Dies at 66," "Nalini Ambady, Psychologist of Intuition, Is Dead at 54," "David Rakoff, Award-Winning Humorist, Dies at 47," "Malik Bendjelloul, 36, Dies; Directed 'Sugar Man' Movie," and "Aaron Swartz, Internet Activist, Dies at 26."

Death in youth is usually worse in most ways than it is in old age, but old age has its challenges, including with regard to death. The older one gets, the less remaining time one can reasonably hope for. Younger people, at least in good health and not facing any external threats, can cope by rationalizing that at least death may not be imminent. That is not a luxury in which the elderly can indulge. One begins to think that one cannot reasonably hope for more than another ten years. Then one's horizon looks more like no more than five years, and then one realizes that the chances of dying within the year are great. One lives knowing that one does not have much time left.[62] The clock is ticking very loudly.

Old age, it is said, is where everybody wants to *get* but nobody wants to *be*. The latter is partly because of the frailties that often accompany advanced age, but the increasing threat of death is another. There is thus a cruel irony here. We want long lives, but the longer we live, the more reason we have to fear that less life remains.[63] This is yet another feature of the human predicament.

6 | Immortality

I do not want to die—no; I neither want to die nor do I want to want to die; I want to live for ever and ever and ever. I want this "I" to live—this poor "I" that I am and that I feel myself to be here and now, and therefore the problem of the duration of my soul, of my own soul, tortures me.

—MIGUEL DE UNAMUNO
The Tragic Sense of Life (Collins, Fontana Library, 1962), 60

Death is bad, but it does not follow from this that being immortal would be good. It is possible that death is bad, but that eternal life would be worse. Thus, we need to ask whether the human predicament would be meliorated or whether it would be exacerbated if we were immortal. The view that immortality would be worse than living for a limited time is one of two broad kinds of optimistic responses to the problem of mortality (that is, one of two ways of rejecting the view that our mortality is part of our predicament). The other kind of optimistic response is to deny, one way or another, that we are (or must remain) mortal.

Delusions and fantasies of immortality

Consider, first, the denial of our mortality. One form this takes is belief in physical resurrection at some future time. If this belief were true, it would make death a kind of suspended animation rather than annihilation. Assuming that the resurrected person would either not die a second time or would be endlessly resurrected after future deaths, this promises a kind of immortality.

Perhaps more common is the belief in an immortal *soul*. The comfort sought here is that though our bodies may die, we shall continue in some—preferably blissful—disembodied state despite our corporeal death and decay.

Such beliefs are instances of wishful thinking. We have no evidence that we shall ever be physically resurrected or that we shall endure as disembodied souls after our physical deaths. Religious texts may speak of these phenomena, but even when they are not waxing poetic and metaphorical, they do not constitute evidence. Indeed, it is much more reasonable to believe that death is annihilation of the self.

Are we really to believe that decomposed, cremated, atomically incinerated, and ingested bodies are to be reconstituted and reanimated? The challenges in understanding the mechanics of this dwarf even other notable problems, such as the logistics of physically accommodating all the resurrected.

These practical problems do not confront the belief in an immortal soul, but that belief faces no shortage of other problems. We have plenty of evidence that our consciousness is a product of our brains. When we are given general anesthesia—administered to our physical bodies and affecting our physical brains—we lose consciousness. When our brains are deprived of oxygen or when we suffer a sufficiently powerful blow to the head, we similarly lose consciousness. It seems unlikely that consciousness, so vulnerable even during life, could then survive the death and decay of our brains. If the response is that our immortal soul is not a continuation of our consciousness, then the promise of an immortal soul seems less like a kind of survival of the self, and thus not very comforting.

Of course, there are those who remain resolute in their belief in either resurrection or the immortality of the soul. In that sense, at least, the issue is unresolved. However, merely because a view has (even vast numbers of) adherents does not mean that it is a reasonable position worth taking seriously. Thus, while I cannot pretend that my comments constitute a full refutation of their view, I do not intend to engage any further with the beliefs that we are immortal in either of these senses. My argument will proceed on the assumption that we are not.

Denial of death is not the preserve of theists and the religious. Atheists are certainly not immune. Among *some* atheists, one optimistic response to the fact of our mortality is to hope that it is a mutable fact. More specifically, there are those who believe that with advancing scientific knowledge, we shall come to understand the process of aging and be able to halt it.

These people, known variably as "life extensionists," "longevists," "(radical) prolongevists,"[1] or even "immortalists," pin their hopes on a range of future knowledge and technologies, including nanotechnology, genetic interventions, anti-aging medications, and cloning body parts to replace failing organs.

It would be unwise to state categorically that *no* extension to current human lifespans is possible or that the quality of extended life would have to be worse than the quality of life currently often is at advanced ages. Nevertheless, it is hard not to see the predicted extent and pace of these developments as a kind of secular millenarianism—an "end of end of days."

For example, inventor and futurist Ray Kurzweil (born in 1948) has said that he has "a very good chance of ... [living] indefinitely."[2] He also claimed (in 2012) that we "will get to a point 15 years from now where, according to [his] models, we will be adding more than a year every year to your remaining life expectancy, where the sands of time are running in rather than running out, where your remaining life expectancy actually stretches out as time goes by."[3] In another pronouncement, he said that although thinking about death is "such a profoundly sad, lonely feeling ... I go back to thinking about how I'm not going to die."[4]

Aubrey de Grey, the chief science officer of the SENS (Strategies for Engineered Negligible Senescence) Research Foundation, is another secular prophet of indefinitely long life. He evidently claimed (in 2002, when he was 49) that he planned to be alive in a hundred years' time,[5] and the subtitle of his co-authored book *Ending Aging* is "The Rejuvenation Breakthroughs That Could *Reverse* Human Aging *in Our Lifetime*."[6]

This kind of optimism has been criticized, but a common response to the critics is to note that the extent and pace of progress has routinely been underestimated by naysayers of the past. Aubrey de Grey, for example, points to the rapid progress from the first powered flight to the first supersonic airliner[7] and rejects what he calls "knee-jerk incredulity"[8] about the prospects of life extension.

Underestimating scientific progress is indeed one kind of error one can make. However, overestimating such progress is another way to err. There are innumerable cases of the latter. Human flight, ironically, is one example. Humans dreamt of this and attempted it for millennia before it became a reality. Conquering mortality is another example. Tales of extreme longevity and of sipping from a fountain of youth have tantalized people for thousands of years, and there has been no shortage of (dubious) advice on life extension.[9] This should at least give pause to those who believe that we are now on the cusp of major life extension.

A promise of indefinitely long life for people in our time—even if that promise is only implicit in confident forecasting—is a seductive gospel for those who are desperate not to age and die. It is something many people want to believe, and many of them may come to believe it at least in part because they want to believe it. Sensationalist prognosticating is thus liable to an ethical critique. It preys on people's vulnerabilities, and it sets people up for disappointment. It is not possible, of course, for those forecasting or believing forecasts of their own indefinite life to find out that they were wrong. However, those who survive them can be delivered such proof. Thus, prophets of boon and their followers can be disappointed by the deaths of those others whom they expected to live indefinitely.

The test of another purportedly life-extending intervention will only be completed in the further future. This intervention, cryonics, aims to preserve those who are declared legally dead but who may not meet a more stringent definition of death—what is known as "information-theoretic" death. On this latter definition, one is only truly dead once it is physically impossible, even with future technologies, to retrieve the person. The idea is that we may be unable to save some people today, but those same people may be salvageable with the use of future technologies. Thus, the person is cryopreserved immediately after legal death in the hope that they can benefit from future medical technologies.

Thus, one postulate of cryonics is that future technologies may be able to save (some) people who cannot be saved now. That postulate is not unreasonable by itself. However, to think that cryonics will help one cheat death, one has to accept a number of other postulates too. First, one has to assume that one will be among those for whom cryopreservation is an option. Those blasted to smithereens, for example, are not candidates for cryopreservation. One also has to presume that one will be among those in whom ischemic damage prior to cryopreservation will not already have caused information-theoretic death.

Further, one has to assume that current (rather than future) cryopreservation technologies are good enough to enable the future rescue technologies to work. For example, one must assume that the cryoprotectants (that is, medical "anti-freeze") used to prevent cell damage during the "vitrification" process are effective in avoiding damage or that the damage can be reversed later.[10]

Another assumption often arises as a result of how expensive cryopreservation is. The expense is partly attributable to the costs of standby teams ready to cryopreserve immediately after legal death, but it is also partly because of the extended period for which people would need to remain cryopreserved. The upshot of the latter is that in some cases, only the head is preserved. This adds a further assumption—that in the future it "is expected that the ability to regrow a new body around a repaired brain will be part of the capabilities of future medicine."[11]

This proliferation of assumptions results in a hope to which only the desperately optimistic can cling. Once again, it would be unwise to say "never"—that cryopreservation could *never* work.

However, hope is misplaced if the odds of what one hopes for are sufficiently slight. Cryopreservation offers a secular version of a bodily resurrection.[12] It offers hope to those who abhor death. Hope brings comfort, but that does not mean that it actually removes one from a predicament.

Even the most deliriously optimistic about conquering death recognize that even if the Holy Grail of halting or reversing aging could be attained, we would not be truly immortal. We could still be killed, either by accident or on purpose. Even if one did not age, one could still die by blunt trauma, stabbing, shooting, gassing, hanging, decapitation, evisceration, or incineration, for example. Just as young, growing people can now die by these means, so could any adult in whom the process of aging had been halted succumb in these ways.

Nor would we be immortal if we could end all accidents and murders. The planet that sustains us will someday become either too cold or too hot to do so. Eventually, the earth will be absorbed by the sun, and the sun will collapse. In the face of these cosmic projections, belief in immortality is outrageously delusional. This has led some to distinguish between "medical immortality" and "true immortality."[13] The former applies when one cannot die from natural causes, while the latter applies when one cannot die from any cause whatsoever.

The phrase "medical *immortality*" is obviously misleading, because those who are merely medically immortal are not immortal at all. They *will* die sooner or later. No matter how small the risk of death by non-natural causes, over the course of eternity, death by such causes can never be avoided. The only question is how long it can be delayed. Thus, the only real immortality is "true immortality." This may be why some optimists have preferred the term "extreme longevity"[14] to "medical immortality."

Although literal immortality is impossible, there are figurative senses in which people can gain "immortality." Thus, for example, people are said to "live on in" or to "gain immortality through" their children and subsequent descendants. Similarly, great artists and writers are said to be immortalized through their works, and people who make other contributions may be immortalized in history books, statues, or by buildings or streets that are named after them.

These are cases in which people make a mark that transcends their own deaths, even though it is neither the case that they themselves literally survive their own deaths nor is it the case that the posthumous mark they leave is one that literally lasts forever (not least because humanity and the earth will not last forever).

It is revealing, therefore, that we even use the term "immortalized" to refer to such cases. It is suggestive that these modest posthumous marks are substitutes for immortality—poor substitutes though they are. They are the best that people can do in the face of their mortality. Woody Allen was clearly aware of this curious "transubstantiation" when he said: "I don't want to achieve immortality through my work ... I want to achieve it through not dying."[15]

Sour grapes

The second optimistic response to our mortality is to deny that its opposite—literal, embodied immortality—would be the good thing that those who hanker after it take it to be. Many of the same arguments could be employed, mutatis mutandis, against the desirability of "extreme longevity," at least if the longevity is sufficiently extreme. However, in what follows I focus on immortality, impossible though that is, for the simple reason that most of the philosophical discussion around this topic has had that focus.

Those who advance arguments that immortality would be bad would certainly deny that they are suffering from a sour-grapes syndrome. In their view, immortality would actually be a bad thing, and we are lucky that our predicament does not include living forever. The "sour grapes" characterization is mine because I think that *under the appropriate conditions* immortality would improve rather than worsen our situation.

The qualification "under the appropriate conditions" is absolutely crucial, because it is not difficult at all to imagine problems with immortality if the only change to the current state of affairs were eliminating the fact that we die. It has long been recognized, for example, that eternal life is worthless if we continue to age and become steadily more decrepit. This was the fate, in Greek mythology, of Tithonus, whose lover, the goddess Eos, asked Zeus to make him immortal. The wish was granted, but because Eos had erred in asking for "eternal life" instead of "eternal youth," Tithonus became increasingly feeble. Jonathan Swift offers a similar cautionary tale in describing the struldbrugs, humans who do not die but do not stop aging.[16]

Those who are considering whether immortality would be a good thing are typically willing to stipulate that the immortal life would have to be one in which one did not lose one's youthful vigor. The problem is that we quickly realize that we have to multiply the number of stipulations required to make immortality (an unqualified) good. We have to heap fantasy upon fantasy, and thus it might be wondered what value this exercise really has.

That is not an unreasonable concern, but the response is that immortality by itself is already a massive counterfactual. If we are to determine whether it would be a good thing, we need to consider other counterfactuals along with it. We are interested in establishing whether there is a possible world in which immortality would be good, even though there are many possible worlds in which it would be bad. To do this, we need to undertake flights of fancy.

In addition to eternal aging, another potential hazard of immortality would be losing one's family and friends to the Grim Reaper. It would certainly be terrible to be bereaved of one's family and close friends. However, this problem is entirely familiar to us as mortals. In the ordinary course of a life, we typically lose our grandparents, then our parents, and then our spouses, siblings, and friends. These are massive losses that we carry with us for the remainder of our own lives. We avoid them only by dying prematurely, in which case, we cause others to be bereaved.

It is true that an immortal life might repeat these experiences. After one has lost one's initial family and friends, one might form new families and friendships only to then suffer the loss of these. However, the obvious solution, once we are stipulating the conditions of immortality, would be to stipulate that immortality is similarly open to one's family and friends.

Indeed, we might stipulate that immortality would be open to *everybody*, for without that stipulation, any number of bad things might occur. The mortals might become jealous of the immortals and might conspire against them. Although the immortals might be immune to death by natural causes, they would not, without further stipulation, be immune to other terrible fates that the mortals might inflict upon them. Alternatively, the barbarities might run in the opposite direction. The immortals might discriminate against the "mere mortals" (giving new meaning to that phrase). Or scarce access to immortality might lead to unfairness. The rich might, quite literally, pay the poor to die for them.

Once we stipulate that immortality would be open to everybody, another very serious problem arises—overpopulation. The earth cannot support an endless proliferation of immortal humans. (Even the current proliferation of mortal humans is a problem, given current rates of consumption.) Humans would continually be added, but the usual rate of subtraction as a result of death would be missing. It would not take long for our planet to become even more crowded than it already is.

There are solutions to this problem. Some are even more fantastical than others. For example, it might be suggested that colonizing other parts of the universe could solve the space problem, but that would only delay the problem.

A more reasonable solution would be to link immortality with non-procreation. One would only become immortal if one desisted from creating new people. (Perhaps imbibing the elixir of life would cause sterility—and would only be effective if taken pre-pubescently, in case you were thinking of breeding and then drinking!) Childlessness might actually become more attractive if immortality became possible, as one would no longer need to "live on in one's children." One could live on, more literally, in oneself.

This particular scenario suggests (but does not strictly imply) immortality first becoming an option for the current generation. However, a better world would have been one without the death-drenched history of ours. Thus, we might imagine a world populated by some initial, immortal but sterile generation. Indeed, that is exactly the vision of the Garden of Eden. According to traditional accounts, mortality was introduced only after (sexual) knowledge and thus reproduction were acquired by the proto-humans, Adam (literally "Man") and Eve (literally "Living One" or "Source of Life").[17] This biblical allegory presciently foreshadows the scientific understanding of the connection between sex and death. Asexual species (such as amoebas) do not die; instead, they divide. Sexually reproducing species die.

There is a further problem. Death is only one of the terrible things that can befall one. We have already stipulated that the immortals would never reach senescence, but plenty of suffering can and does befall those still in their youth or (what under current conditions we call) middle age. Thus, we would have to stipulate either that the immortal life would be a blissful one or that immortality would be a reversible option. The latter would allow somebody to opt out of immortality and to die if he or she found the quality of life to be unbearable.

We should not underestimate the difficulty of exercising an option to die, which is one reason why an eternally blissful life would be so preferable. However, exercising an option to die is not a net disadvantage relative to our current mortal state, because poor quality of life already leads many people to want to die earlier than they otherwise would. It is true, of course, that an immortal exercising an option to die would be losing out on much more life than a mortal who decides to end life earlier than it otherwise would have ended. In this way, the decision may be more momentous for the immortal. However, that disadvantage of immortality would need to be weighed against the disadvantage, on the other side, of being involuntarily mortal. When one does that, immortality seems to be a net gain.

Although (analytic) philosophers have written about the foregoing worries pertaining to immortality, these are not the issues that have exercised them much. Instead, most of their attention has been focused on the argument that an immortal life would be a life of boredom. Bernard Williams is the most prominent exponent of this argument.[18]

He claims that two conditions would need to be met in order for immortality to be good for me. First, it must be *I* who lives forever. Second, the state in which I survive would have to be one that is attractive to me.[19] He argues that the second condition would not be met in an immortal life because one would inevitably become bored by an endless repetition of the same experiences. He recognizes that one way to avoid this problem would be "survival by means of an indefinite series of lives."[20] However, that possibility violates the first condition, he says. The future selves would have to be sufficiently different from me not to be bored by the experiences that would have come to bore me. However, any future selves that were so different would no longer be I. If, by contrast, those future selves were sufficiently close to my self that it was I who survived, then the boredom I would experience would kill the desire to go on living. Thus, immortality would not be good.

It is interesting that this argument has precipitated so much more philosophical interest than the others, for it seems that it invites the same sort of response as the others, namely, stipulating another condition that would be necessary for immortality to be desirable. The condition this time would be that our immortal selves would not become bored with our never-ending lives. This need not be the very strong claim that we would experience *no* boredom. Even in mortal lives, the presence of *some* boredom is not thought to make it the case that we would be better off dead.[21] Thus, the condition we need to stipulate is that one would not become bored with one's immortal life as a whole. Put another way, if we did experience any boredom, it would need to be sufficiently limited as not to impose a serious burden.

Perhaps even that is a lot to stipulate, but it certainly does not seem to be any more fantastical than the other conditions that are readily accepted in hypothetically evaluating immortality. An immortal life without overwhelming boredom is no harder to imagine than an immortal life of youthful vigor that is devoid of any serious suffering, for example. In fact, it seems a lot easier to imagine.

Bernard Williams appears to think that there is an important difference between the boredom objection and other possible problems with immortality. He says that whereas the other issues are contingencies, the tedium problem is not.[22] However, the case he makes for this claim is not convincing. For example, it seems to be premised on the assumption that the immortal person would be "living as an embodied person in the *world rather as it is.*"[23] That assumption simply cannot hold, given the conglomeration of far-fetched hypotheticals we are considering. Thus, it seems that we could just stipulate the absence of (significant) boredom as a condition for the desirability of immortality.

However, even without stipulating further departures from "the world rather as it is," it is actually not that difficult to imagine the condition being met. This is supported by the arguments of some of those who have criticized Professor Williams's claim that an immortal life would be a tedious and meaningless one.

For example, John Martin Fischer has noted that although many experiences are "self-exhausting," enough are "repeatable" to avoid boredom taking root in an immortal life.[24] Self-exhausting experiences, as the name suggests, are those that we do not care to repeat many times, if at all. They include not only disappointing experiences but also pleasing experiences that one only wants to have done once or perhaps a few times. We could certainly tire of these experiences even within a finite life. However, many other experiences are repeatable. These include "the pleasures of sex, of eating fine meals and drinking fine wines, of listening to beautiful music, of seeing great art, and so forth."[25] Humans can repeat these experiences many times in a mortal life, and there seems no reason why they should tire of them in an immortal life either.

Part of the secret, of course, is not to have the same experience in an endless loop. The experiences are repeatable in part because they are spaced apart. Better lives contain a wide array of repeatable positive experiences. One has each at intervals.[26] With these sorts of patterns, people do not tend to tire of the experiences during life—unless ill health or decrepitude saps their ability to enjoy them. However, the immortal life we are imagining is one in which health and vigor are retained.

It is true that some experiences that were once repeatable may cease to be. Perhaps one loses one's interest in a particular genre of fiction or one ceases to enjoy a particular person's company. However, in such cases, new interests and friendships often emerge, providing new repeatable experiences.

Bernard Williams's worry about these evolving interests and values is that eventually the constellation of valued experiences will be so different that even if the person is the same at vastly different times, he would not value at an earlier time the things he values at the much later time. Knowing this in advance, he would not find the life of his distant future self to be attractive. This, says Professor Williams, violates the second of the conditions that are necessary for immortality to be desirable.

A number of authors have rightly been critical of this argument. They have noted that our characters, preferences, and values can change over the course of even a mortal life.[27] Indeed, one's preferences and values typically change quite considerably between childhood and adulthood. The priorities, desires, and values of a toddler are not those of the middle-aged person, for example. Thus Professor Williams's argument would seem to imply that living to middle age holds no attraction for the toddler and thus is not a good thing for that toddler.

This is a *reductio ad absurdum* of the *reductio ad tedium*. Toddlers do have an interest in living to middle age despite the changes in their values, goals, and preferences. This is partly because the changes are gradual. The four-year-old's values, goals, and preferences are very similar to those of the five-year-old she becomes, and the latter are in turn very similar to those of the six-year-old she becomes, and so on. Thus, at each stage, the person has an interest in surviving even though over a sufficiently long period, it comes to be the case that one's values, goals, and preferences are very different from when one was much younger.

If the years have done what they should do, one's later self is more experienced, more mature, more considered. In that case, one might cringe at the thought of one's earlier self, but that does not mean that it would have been better to have died before that maturation took place. There is no reason why the same should not be true in an immortal life.

Of course, sometimes the additional years make a person worse rather than better. In extreme cases, an innocent child becomes a moral monster. However, even over the course of an eternal life, one does not have to become, at some stage, an Adolf Hitler or a Joseph Stalin.[28] Instead, the ordinary trajectories of maturation in a mortal life could continue in an immortal one. There is no reason to think that one would have to cycle through despicable personalities, the appearances of whom might make our earlier deaths preferable.

Although Professor Williams's argument is aimed at the conclusion that an immortal life would be a *boring* one, he also says in a few places that it would be a meaningless one.[29] However, unless one takes a boring life to be meaningless, it is not clear that he actually provides any argument at all for the claim that an immortal life would be meaningless. Perhaps it seems obvious to many people that a boring life would indeed be meaningless. It certainly is not obvious to me. Any number of boring tasks may be meaningful (from the perspectives at which meaning is attainable). For example, repeatedly performing safety checks on airplanes may be boring, but it certainly is not meaningless (from relevant human perspectives). Similarly, performing many of the tasks that are necessary to care for a young child—feeding, cleaning, and changing—can become boring, but they are very meaningful from the perspective of the relevant child, parent, and family.

Thus, it does not seem that Professor Williams's argument is in fact about the *meaninglessness* of an immortal life. This does not mean that there are no arguments for the conclusion that an immortal life would be meaningless. One such argument claims that in an immortal life, there would be no sense of urgency to achieve anything. If one knew that one would live forever, there would be no rush to do the things that make a mark. One could sit back, knowing that there was plenty of time to do those things. This deferral would be repeated endlessly with the upshot that one did nothing worthwhile.

This concern is not convincing despite the fact that a genuinely immortal being, having no temporal limit, would have no need to transcend such a limit. However, insofar as that is the case, the absence of a temporally transcendent meaning would not be bad. Mortals live in the shadow of death, which cuts short our projects. We may succeed in leaving some mark on the world, but in time, that too is obliterated by the passage of time. Immortals would simply not have this problem. While mortals may yearn for temporally transcendent meaning, immortals may have no such need, but then the absence of such meaning would not be bad for them. This is not to say that their lives would be meaningless. The meaning would simply not have to come from transcending an absent temporal limit.

A temporally unlimited being could nonetheless have other limits, and we can well imagine meaning being sought through an attempt to transcend those other limits, including spatial limits and limits of significance. Even if there were no urgency to do so, there may nonetheless be a desire to do so. They may want to make a difference and enjoy doing so. No urgency would be required, as the desire would motivate them even in the absence of urgency. This is because urgency is not the only motivator. Non-urgent need is another, but so is desire. Often in our lives, there is no urgency to eat or to relax, but we do those things because we like to do them. Similarly, captive primates that do not have to worry about finding food actually prefer to forage for their food than to have it presented on a platter. They do not *have* to forage, but they *want* to.

Nor need we be concerned by the claim that an immortal life would "lack any meaningful shape or pattern."[30] Indeed, it is difficult to make sense of what exactly this concern is. Geoffrey Scarre says that "it would resemble an infinitely long river that meandered eternally without ever reaching the sea. There would be no arch-shaped structure of birth, growth, maturing, decline and death.... It would be a life that was going nowhere specific...."[31]

These are all metaphors, of course, that only make the concern harder to decode. What exactly is wrong with a meandering river that never reaches the sea? And why is it thought that it has no (meaningful) shape? Its shape is formed by the contours it takes. What it lacks is not shape but an end, yet this is precisely what is attractive to those who do not want the "ride" to the finish. Those who abhor our mortality do not like the kind of arch to which Professor Scarre refers. They can do without the decline and death that complete the arch by battering and then annihilating us. It is really difficult to see why anybody should want his or her life to take *that* shape.

Conclusion

Being mortal causes many humans considerable anxiety. The shadow of death looms over our lives. No matter who we are, where and when we live, and what we do, each of us knows that he or she is doomed to die. We first gain this terrifying awareness as quite young children. Insofar as we can, we put this fact out of our consciousness, but it lurks beneath the surface, breaking through at times when we cannot but confront our mortality. This awareness is one of the chief triggers of existential angst, and it spurs attempts to find meaning. Our mortality is an unbearable limit that we seek to transcend. Yet it is an ultimate limit that we simply cannot transcend in any literal way. We are not the only mortals, but as far as we know, we are the mortals with the most acute sense of their own mortality. Mortality is thus a brute and ugly feature of the human predicament.

However, if an immortal version of our current lives were possible, it would not be a good thing. For example, we would age progressively and suffer increasingly. Moreover, if immortality were widespread, the earth would rapidly become even more overpopulated than it already is.

That should not lead us to think that immortality per se would be bad. Under specific conditions, eternal life would be better than the mortal life we lead. In other words, mortality is only one feature of the human predicament. Substituting mortality with immortality, while holding other features of the human predicament constant, would extend the predicament temporally and would also introduce novel features unless we imposed the kinds of conditions I have discussed. However, if we imagine immortal lives under these stipulated conditions, it would be much better than our current mortal condition, or so I have argued.

Those who disagree with this conclusion and persist in maintaining that immortality would be a bad, should not seek solace in their view. Even if immortality would be bad, it does not follow that it would not be good to live longer. It is possible that while immortality would be bad, it would be better to live much longer than we actually do. Nor does it follow that mortality is good. It is possible that we are damned if we die *and* damned if we don't. Some predicaments are that intractable. Perhaps it would have been best, as I believe, never to have been at all. After all, those who never exist are in no condition, let alone any predicament. They are not doomed to die. And if one thinks that an eternal life under the best conditions constitutes a kind of doom, they are also not doomed to live for eternity.

7 | Suicide

> There is but one truly serious philosophical problem, and that is suicide.
>
> —ALBERT CAMUS
> *The Myth of Sisyphus, Translated by Justin O'Brien*
> *(London: Penguin, 1975), 1*

Introduction

Even if we do not agree with Albert Camus that suicide is the *only* truly philosophical problem, we should certainly acknowledge that it is *a* serious philosophical problem. Taking one's own life is a momentous act, not least because of its finality. One cannot undo a suicide. One annihilates oneself. Yet, contrary to what some have thought, suicide cannot for this reason be ruled out categorically. There are some fates that are both worse than and only avoidable by death.

We cannot state baldly that the human predicament is such a fate,[1] and thus suicide cannot be recommended to all people at all times as a solution to the human predicament. One reason for this, as we saw in chapter 5, is that death (which obviously includes death by one's own hand) is part of the human predicament. One's death obviously does not solve the problem of one's mortality. Second, suicide, like death more generally, does not typically solve the problem of meaninglessness.

Indeed, it often exacerbates that problem. Death *can* solve the problem of *felt* meaninglessness. Once one is dead, one can no longer suffer the feeling that one's life lacks meaning. However, as I shall argue, there are often other, less drastic responses to that problem.

Although suicide (like death more generally) does not solve the human predicament in its entirety, there are situations in which it becomes a reasonable response to one's condition. These are situations in which the quality of life becomes so poor that life is not worth continuing.[2] A felt sense of meaningless can contribute to this, but it is not the only consideration.

Yet many people condemn suicide even in situations in which the quality of life has become quite appalling. This has not always been the case. Some cultures have been relatively accepting of suicide and even regarded it as virtuous in some circumstances. The opposite is true of many other cultures, including most contemporary Western cultures. In those societies that frown upon suicide, it is generally either morally condemned or pathologized. This view is partly correct and partly mistaken. It is quite clear that suicide *often* results from psychopathology or is morally wrong. Nevertheless, suicide has been the subject of more opprobrium than is warranted. I shall argue that although suicide is always *tragic* (because it always involves serious costs), we ought to be less judgmental about it, whether psychiatrically or morally, than people usually are. Suicide is sometimes a reasonable—even the most reasonable—response to a particular human's predicament (rather than to the human predicament in general). To this end, I shall argue against the view that suicide is always (or almost always) wrong before discussing the situations in which it is and is not justified.

I hasten to add that my defense of suicide is highly qualified. One cannot write in support of (some instances of) suicide without considering the possibility that some desperate person might read one's words, ignore the qualifications, and act precipitously in ending his or her life. This thought creates a huge emotional burden. One does not want to be the philosophical equivalent—in effect rather than intent—of the callous mob yelling "jump" to the distressed person on a ledge. At the same time, one wants to speak in defense of those suicides who have acted reasonably but who have been condemned or pathologized for taking their own lives. One also wants to extend a hand of understanding to those who find themselves in so appalling a condition that, despite the serious costs of death, it is actually in their best interests, all things considered. And one wants to declare that things are the way one thinks that they are, disturbing though that may be. The self-help that is dished out in heaps is insulting to those who are in extremis. We need frank but compassionate talk about these difficult matters.

Although analytic philosophers have said much about suicide, their focus has been almost exclusively on the question whether suicide is ever morally permissible, as distinct from whether there is ever something stronger to be said in its favor. Moreover, most (but not all) such philosophical writing considers this question within the context of terminal disease or unbearable and intractable (usually physical) suffering.[3]

For some, these are the only bases for suicide that are even worthy of discussion. Others are prepared to extend the discussion to a limited range of other cases, such as those involving irreversible loss of dignity. Suicide on any other grounds, according to this view, must surely be wrong. I take this view to be mistaken. We cannot preclude the possibility that somebody's life may become unacceptably burdensome to him even though his death is not already imminent and he is not suffering the most extreme and intractable physical pain or irreversible loss of dignity.

Not all who have ignored other grounds have done so because they think that such suicide would be impermissible. Some of them may have decided, given the general antipathy to suicide, to focus on the conditions under which suicide can most easily be defended. This approach, although understandable, is regrettable. If an autonomous person's life is unacceptably burdensome to him, then suicide is a reasonable topic for discussion even though others might not find life in the same condition unacceptably burdensome. Such suicide is worthy of consideration even though it is more controversial than suicide in the circumstances that are usually discussed.

Therefore, my discussion of suicide will be broader than usual. I shall examine suicide as a response not only to the worst conditions in which people sometimes find themselves, but also to less severe conditions that might nevertheless be reasonably judged to make life not worth continuing. These include less drastic physical conditions, psychological suffering of varying degrees, as well as lesser indignities, including (at least for adults) dependence on others for the performance of basic tasks such as feeding and bathing oneself. I shall also discuss suicide as a response to meaninglessness in life.

In addition to looking at a broader range of conditions to which suicide may be a response, I also plan to examine not only the question whether suicide is permissible, but also whether there is something more to be said for it, at least in some circumstances. In this regard, I shall not be concerned with the question whether it is ever *required*, but rather with the question whether it may sometimes be *more* rational than continuing to live.

Although my discussion of suicide will be broader than usual in these ways, there is one way in which what I say will have a narrower focus. I shall not be concerned with the question whether suicide ought to be legally permissible or the conditions under which it should be legally permissible. My focus will be on an ethical and rational evaluation of suicide. This will have relevance to normative questions about the law. For example, insofar as suicide is not immoral, one cannot use its purported immorality to justify a legal prohibition. However, demonstrating that suicide is morally permissible (or even preferable) is not sufficient to show that it should be legal. To reach that conclusion, one would have to ward off other arguments for attaching legal sanctions to suicide. I happen to think that suicide should be legal, but I shall not argue for that here.[4]

Nor shall I be concerned with questions about what suicide is. To be sure, there are cases where it is unclear whether the term "suicide" is suitably applied. For example, was Socrates' death a suicide?[5] He did drink (raise to his lips, sip, and swallow) the poisonous hemlock that resulted in his death. Yet, he did so because he was sentenced to death, a penalty inflicted by means of the ingestion of hemlock. He did not want to die and was not aiming at his death. Was Captain Lawrence Oates's death suicide? A member of Robert Falcon Scott's expedition to the South Pole, he realized on the ill-fated return journey that his injury was slowing down and thus endangering his comrades' safe return to base camp. They would not abandon him. One day, he stepped out into the snow. His aim was to relieve the burden on his comrades rather than to die, but he knew that his action would result in his death. Fascinating though these questions are, my interest here is in paradigmatic cases of suicide where somebody kills himself because he takes that to be in his own interests, all things considered. Although there may be some sense in which such people would rather not die, they do, given their circumstances, want to die. If these cases of self-interested self-killing are not suicide, then there are no suicides. My concern is with the evaluation rather than the definition of suicide.

Discussions about the ethics of suicide are immediately biased by the verb that customarily attaches to it in English. One "commits" suicide. Since this presupposes the wrongfulness of suicide, I shall avoid that verb, opting instead for "carry out" suicide. This is evaluatively neutral, avoiding both the usual bias against suicide and the unusual bias in favor of it that the verb "achieve" would indicate. "Carry out" is preferable to "practice," which implies something ongoing. Finally, "carry out" also implies a suicide that is completed rather than merely attempted.

When successful, suicide results in death. Some believe that life continues after death. Others take death to be the irreversible cessation of the self. Which of these views is true is relevant to an evaluation of suicide. If, for example, there were life after death, then we would need to know just what that life were like. It would make a difference if death were followed by torments still worse than those experienced in earthly life or if it were followed by blissful pleasures of which the pre-dead could only dream. I shall assume, as I did in chapter 5, that there is no afterlife and that death is the end. Those who reject this assumption and wish to evaluate suicide face the unenviable task of demonstrating, rather than merely asserting, what the nature of the purported afterlife is.

In the next section, I shall respond to a number of arguments that are commonly advanced against suicide, arguments that are intended to show that suicide is never (or almost never) justified. Having shown that these arguments fail and that suicide is sometimes permissible, I shall venture in the following section to even more controversial terrain. There I shall argue that, all things considered, suicide may be a reasonable response to particular humans' predicaments much more often than people think (even though it does not solve all features of those predicaments).

Responding to common arguments against suicide

Suicide as murder

Some have regarded suicide as a species of murder and as heinous. The word "murder," unlike "killing," is not value-neutral. It denotes wrongfulness (or, in the legal context, unlawfulness). Thus, everybody, or at least everybody who understands the concept, thinks that murder is wrong. The disagreement arises with regard to *why* murder is wrong and thus which killings do or do not constitute murder.

If, for example, one thinks that murder is wrong because it involves taking an innocent human life, then it does indeed follow that suicide is (usually) wrong. However, assuming that the taking of innocent human life is wrong merely begs the question. Those who think that suicide is sometimes permissible clearly do not accept this assumption. More specifically, they deny that suicide can be faulted merely because the person killing himself is killing an innocent human. If we ask ourselves *why* it is usually wrong to kill innocent humans, we find that there may be grounds for distinguishing suicide from murder.

One compelling explanation of why murder is wrong is that it thwarts interests that the victims have a right to have respected.[6] If that is so, then suicide may be permissible when two conditions are met: (1) Continued life is not in a person's best interest; and (2) the relevant right, the right to life, does not preclude taking that person's life. These conditions are typically met in cases of rational suicide. In such cases, life has become so burdensome that continued life is either not in that person's interests or not reasonably thought to be in his interests. Moreover, since the person who dies is competent and has consented to be killed—for that is what rationally killing oneself implies—the right to life has not been violated.

There is more than one way to understand why one's right to life is not violated when one kills oneself. If one understands rights in such a way that the correlative duties are borne only by those other than the right-bearer, then the right-bearer has no duty to him- or herself. On this view, my having a negative right to life implies that others have correlative duties not to kill me. It does not imply that I have a duty not to kill myself. Thus, when a person rationally kills himself, he has not violated his own rights.

Those who think that a right's correlative duties include a reflexive duty on the right-bearer will say that my right not to be killed includes a duty on me not to kill myself. However, even that view does not entail the wrongfulness of suicide. This is because a competent right-bearer has the moral power either to assert or waive a right. I have rights to my property, but I may waive these rights by lending something I own. I have a right to bodily integrity, but I may waive this when I grant a surgeon permission to perform a procedure on me. If a right-bearer were to lack such power, then the right, rather than serving the interests of the right-bearer, could become his master. Thus, even if rights entail correlative duties to self, these duties differ in a fundamental way from other duties correlated to the right. Unlike other duties, reflexive duties are duties from which the duty-bearer may release himself (because he is the right-bearer who has the power to waive the right.) It is because of this that the second view of rights, which claims that rights have correlative reflexive duties, reduces to the first view of rights, which denies they have correlative reflexive duties. The first view is thus preferable because it is theoretically more parsimonious than the second view.

Opponents of suicide may argue in response that because basic rights, such as a negative right to life, are inalienable, a right-bearer may not release himself or others from the correlative duty. The assumption that basic rights are inalienable is controversial. One reason for disputing it is that, if rights are inalienable, then they become a burden rather than a benefit to the right-bearer. However, the permissibility of suicide does not rest on rejecting the claim that rights are inalienable. Those who think that suicide is sometimes permissible or reasonable could accept that rights are inalienable. They then need only distinguish between the inalienability of a right and its waivability. To alienate a right always involves ceasing to have it. Although waiving a right sometimes has the same effect,[7] it is usually more limited. To waive a right may involve only forgoing its protection at a given time in a particular circumstance and with regard to a particular correlative duty-bearer. Thus, if I alienate my right not to be killed, anybody may kill me at any time. I no longer enjoy the moral protection of the right, and I cannot regain it. However, if I merely waive my right with respect to a particular person, I release that person— either myself in the case of suicide or another in the case of euthanasia[8]—from the duty not to kill me.[9] If somebody else kills me, he has violated my right because he was not within the scope of my right-waiving. And if I change my mind, I can reassert my right and thereby reimpose the duty on the person whom I had released from the duty.

It follows from this that we do not need to postulate an independent negative right to die in order to defend the permissibility of suicide. All we need to do is understand that a right not to be killed has a corollary—the permission to kill oneself.

Given this, some opponents of suicide might deny that the wrongfulness of murder is best explained as a violation of a right to life. They may argue instead that murder is wrong because it violates a duty to God rather than to the person who is killed. However, this argument suffers from the usual sorts of problems faced by religious arguments. Most important, the underlying assumptions are highly controversial. These include not only the claim that God exists but also, if he does, that the prohibition on murder includes a prohibition on suicide. Given that the burdens endured by those who contemplate suicide are more easily demonstrable than are the assumptions of the religious argument, the former should weigh more heavily than the latter, at least for those who do not share the assumptions. To suggest otherwise is to condemn the suicidal to an unbearable predicament on grounds that cannot be verified.

Suicide as irrational

The argument that a right to life, because it can be waived, entails a permission to die presupposes that the right-bearer is competent to make the decision whether to waive the right. Some critics of suicide have implicitly denied that those who would kill themselves are competent to make this decision. This, say the critics, is because all suicide is irrational. Thus, anybody who kills himself cannot be competent.

The claim that all suicide is irrational can be understood in different ways, corresponding to different senses of irrationality. One way in which somebody might be irrational is by adopting means that do not (and cannot reasonably be thought to) secure their ends. Thus, for example, to attempt to quench one's thirst by shaving one's head is irrational because head-shaving is obviously not an appropriate means to quenching one's thirst. By contrast, drinking a glass of water is rational because it is clearly one means of attaining one's end. Following this ends-means view of rationality (and irrationality), some suicides clearly are irrational. Suicide is not an effective means to every end. Thus, when it does not serve one's end, it is irrational. However, it should be equally clear that suicide may also often be entirely rational under the ends-means conception of rationality. If one's end is to avoid those of life's burdens that can only be avoided by the cessation of one's life, then suicide is rational.

Perhaps, then, the suicide critics' conception of irrationality is different. Perhaps they understand as irrational any end to which suicide is the means. On this view, suicide is irrational not because it is a hopelessly ineffective means to attaining the desired goal, but rather because it is a means to an irrational end. Although it may be rational, as a means, to kill oneself if one wants to die, it is not rational to want to die.

If the claim is that it is never (or even almost never) rational to want to die, then again it is difficult to sustain. It implies that life is *never* (or almost never) so bad that death is preferable to continued life in such a condition. This view must certainly be a dogma rather than an informed response to the range of horrific conditions in which humans can and regularly do find themselves. These include excruciating pains that when palliated (if suitable medications are available[10]) are alleviated only by dulling one's consciousness and thereby diminishing one's independence and exacerbating one's indignity. They also include terminal diseases that steadily sap one's life, and irreversible degenerative conditions that cause an inexorable loss of either one's mind or the use of one's body. And we should not forget those who suffer grinding poverty or massive injuries and hideous disfigurements, and those who are paralyzed or who irreversibly lose bowel or bladder control. Although not everybody in such situations would rather die than continue to live in such a condition, the preference of those who would rather die is not unreasonable.

This refutes the suggestion that those who are suffering the burdens of life are not in a fit state to judge whether death is preferable to continued life. Those burdens do not cloud the mind, rendering sound judgment impossible. Instead, the burdens are entirely germane to decisions about whether life is worth continuing. Indeed, in such circumstances, the burdens may not so much cloud the mind as focus it.

Suicide as unnatural

Closely related to the claim that suicide is irrational is the objection that it is unnatural. The argument that a practice is immoral because it is unnatural occurs in many contexts, but it is deeply flawed and succumbs to well-known objections. There are at least two ways in which suicide is said to be unnatural. First, suicide leads to one's dying sooner than one would have died if nature had been allowed to take its course. Second, suicide is contrary to the natural instinct to continue living.

The first version of the argument assumes that a person's taking his or her own life is not part of nature. It assumes, therefore, that the actions of moral agents are not natural in the relevant sense. That is a controversial claim, but we may grant it for the moment. If suicide were morally problematic because it leads to an earlier death than would naturally have occurred, then saving lives, at least those not threatened by moral agents, is also morally problematic because it also subverts a person's natural fate.[11] It leads him to die later than he would have died if nature had been allowed to take its course. There are some people who are willing to embrace this conclusion, but most see it as a *reductio ad absurdum* of the argument. Those who are prepared to accept the implication for saving lives need to explain why it is immoral to alter the time that one would naturally have died. What normative force does nature have? And if nature does have such force, why may we interfere with nature in other ways, by building houses or farming, for example?

The second version of the argument is not any better. Although humans (like other animals) do have a natural instinct to continue living, it is also the case in some circumstances that people naturally lose the will to continue living. It is also not clear why we ought to comply with our natural instincts. Instincts to violence and sex are regularly thought to be instincts that should be kept in check, even by those who think that we ought not act in a contrary way to the instinct to continue living.

Suicide as cowardice

A fourth way in which suicide is criticized is by claiming that it is a cowardly act. The idea is that the person who kills himself lacks the courage to face life's burdens and thus "takes the easy way out." Courage, on this view, requires standing one's ground in the face of life's adversities and bearing them with fortitude.

One way to respond to this criticism is to deny that accepting life's burdens is always courageous. This will seem odd to those who have a crude conception of courage according to which the unswerving, fearless response to adversity is always courageous. More sophisticated accounts of courage, however, recognize that a steely response may sometimes be a failing. This is what lies behind the adage that sometimes "discretion is the better part of valor." On the more sophisticated views, too much bravado ceases to be courageous and is instead foolhardiness or even foolishness. Once we recognize that courage should not be confused with its simulacra, the possibility arises that some of life's burdens may be so great and the point of bearing them so tenuous that enduring them further is not courageous at all and may even be foolish.

Simply because a suicidal person judges death to be less bad than continued existence does not mean that bringing about his own death is *easy*. There is obviously a sense in which he has judged it to be *easier* than continuing to live, but that sort of relative claim can be made, in the reverse direction, by the person who judges continued life in a burdensome condition to be less bad than the alternative of taking his own life. Yet the advocate of the cowardice objection does not claim that the one who endures life's burdens is, for that reason, cowardly. That one option is preferable to another does not mean that the preferred option is *easy*.

Indeed, neither living with significant burdens nor taking one's own life is without difficulty. Although one may be judged preferable to the other, it is preferable in the sense of being "less bad," rather than "more good."

Those who accuse suicides of cowardice fail to see just how demanding the task of killing oneself can be. Suicide is difficult because of the formidable life drive that animates most people, even most of those who eventually take their own lives.

Even if some people lose *all* will to live, many others who kill themselves would like to continue living if it were not so burdensome. They have to overcome their will to live in order to take their lives. This is not easy at all. It is thus unsurprising that more people contemplate suicide than attempt it, and there are more attempted suicides than successful ones.

Given the resolve that some people have to muster in order to take their own lives, combined with the futility or severity of their circumstances, it may well be that suicide is—at least sometimes—the more courageous option than remaining alive.

Interests of others

A fifth critique of suicide is that the person who kills himself violates duties he has to others. In earlier times, suicide was not only morally condemned but also criminalized because the person who took his own life thereby deprived the king of one of his subjects.[12] Thus, suicide was viewed as a kind of theft against the monarch. Today, this view seems at best quaint, but more likely repugnant, because it implies the king's ownership of his subjects. The idea can be made more palatable to modern sensibilities if one shifts from speaking of the king's ownership of his subjects to the state's interest in the life of the citizen. However, this version of the view seems harder pressed to rule out all suicide. Even if the state does have an interest in each of its citizens, it is surely the case that the interest each citizen has in himself is going to outweigh the state's interest in him. If his life has become so burdensome to him that continued life is not in his interests, it is hard to see how the state's interest in his continued life would be sufficient to render suicide wrong. This is not to suggest that there could be no such circumstances,[13] but they could hardly be the norm.

The argument that suicide may violate duties to others assumes its strongest form when the relevant others are close family, friends, or sometimes others to whom one has special obligations. These sorts of people stand to suffer profound loss if one takes one's own life. One's family and friends are bereaved, but the loss may be heightened by the fact that one took one's own life. This may be exacerbated by feelings of guilt that they may experience over one's suicide. Moreover, one's death may preclude fulfilling duties that one had toward them. One's children may be deprived of a parent and the fulfillment of one's parental duties (even if one's spouse remains alive). One's friends may be deprived of one's company or counsel, and one's patients, clients, or students may be deprived of one's care, services, or instruction.[14] For these reasons, some people have been inclined to view suicide as selfish. The suicide is said to think only of herself and not those who are left behind.

As was the case with the earlier arguments, this one is inadequate to rule out all suicide. There probably are suicides where the person who kills herself has given her own interests excessive weight relative to the interests of others. Some burdens of life are insufficient to defeat the duties one owes to others. Suicide in such circumstances may indeed be selfish. But this is surely not always the case. The greater the burdens of a life, the less likely it is that the interests of friends and family will carry sufficient moral weight to defeat the prospective suicide's interest in ceasing to exist. It would be indecent, for example, for family members to expect a loved one to remain alive in conditions of extreme pain or degradation. In such circumstances, it is unlikely that she would be able, even if she remained alive, to fulfill many or most of her duties to them. Although they will miss her presence if she dies, her condition is too burdensome to require her continued presence. In such circumstances, what is selfish is the insistence that the prospective suicide remain alive, not that she seeks her own demise.

The argument about selfishness can backfire in another way. Just as it is sometimes the case that those who kill themselves have accorded insufficient weight to the interests of others, so it is sometimes the case that those who *do not* kill themselves make this error. Consistent with what I have already said, I do not think that the interests of others are decisive. Nevertheless, there are situations in which a person's net interest in continued life is negligible, because she will die soon anyway and the quality of her life is appalling. If seeing out her days, rather than taking her own life earlier, would spell financial ruin for her family (due to the costs of her medical care), then it may well be unduly selfish not to take one's own life.

The finality of death

Finally, there is the finality argument. From the indisputable premise that death is final or irreversible, some people infer that for this reason we should not carry out suicide. This argument takes a number of forms.

One version of the argument notes that there are alternatives to death that do not close off options in the way that suicide does. Thus, one might try to enjoy life despite the burdens, perhaps by trying to distract oneself. This need not involve becoming oblivious to the burdens, but rather by seeking relief in not dwelling on them. A second possible response is to accept life's burdens and endure them quietly or perhaps ironically. A third response is to protest against one's predicament (even though doing so cannot possibly undo or even ameliorate that predicament). What distinguishes this response from mere acceptance is that protest is a kind of *intolerance* of one's predicament. When others are responsible for one's burdens, one could protest against them. However, one's protests need not be directed at anybody. It can be a generalized anger about an unfortunate state of affairs for which nobody is (proximately) responsible. (Ultimately, even if not proximately, one's parents are responsible for one's human predicament. It was they who placed one in it. Yet many people, even those who resent their predicaments, are not inclined to bear any resentment toward their parents. This may be because of a close, loving relationship between parent and offspring, or because the offspring recognize that the parents did not know better when they procreated.)

There is indeed something to be said for each of these nonlethal responses to life's burdens, and thus one or another of them may well be the most appropriate response in some circumstances. For example, if one's burdens are, for the moment, relatively minor and the costs of suicide (to others or oneself) are great, then enjoying one's life despite the burdens may indeed be the most reasonable reaction. If the burdens are greater but still bearable, and carrying out suicide would impose yet greater burdens on those to whom one is obligated, then acceptance of (and sometimes even protest against) one's condition may be preferable. However, noting these alternatives is insufficient to show that they are always preferable to suicide. If one's condition is bad enough, then it may make no sense to continue living, even if continued life enabled one to continue protesting. Why continue to bear and even to protest an unbearable condition if one could bring it to an end, albeit by bringing oneself to an end?

A second version of the finality argument notes an interesting difference between suicide and the other options. If one kills oneself, then there is no opportunity to change one's mind later and choose one of the other options instead. By contrast, if one chooses one of the nonlethal alternatives, one can at any time reverse one's decision and choose another course, including suicide.

Recognizing this is important for understanding the momentous nature of a suicide decision. However, an action cannot be judged unacceptable merely because it is irreversible. First, if we always deferred to a reversible course of action, then there is one sense in which the reversible decision becomes irreversible. That is to say, if one should never choose a course of action that cannot be reversed, then at each juncture that one reconsiders, one is precluded from choosing suicide and thus one may never really switch to suicide from one of the nonlethal responses to life's burdens. If one may never switch to suicide, then though one may change one's mind and shift from one non-suicidal response to another, opting for a non-suicidal response becomes irreversible. Second, and more important, there is nothing about irreversible decisions that preclude their being the best decisions. We only have to be extra sure, when making such decisions, that they are the right ones.

A third version of the finality argument states that while one is alive, there is still hope that one's condition may improve, whereas once one is dead, all hope is lost. One problem with this version is that it often misses the point of suicide. The person who carries out suicide need not think that his condition will *not* be alleviated. He may merely judge his current condition to be unacceptable and conclude that, no matter how much his situation may improve later, that outcome is simply not worth what he would have to endure in the interim. Moreover, even when the decision to kill oneself is based on a judgment about one's future prospects, it is not always rational to err on the side of continued life. Sometimes, there is no realistic hope of improvement. In such situations, one may be faced with a choice between the remotest of possibilities that one's condition will improve and the certainty that one will suffer terrible burdens in the interim. Those who wager rationally do not consider only the quality of the competing options but also their probability. At least sometimes, then, suicide may be appropriate even when not all hope has been lost.

Broadening the case for suicide

So far, I have argued that suicide is sometimes rational and permissible. Given the number of people who think that suicide is always irrational and wrong, these arguments are important. However, they support only a very modest claim. It is also a claim that many others have already defended. In what follows, I shall defend some more extensive claims. I shall argue that suicide is permissible and reasonable more often than is widely thought.

A more accurate assessment of life's quality

Central to judgments about the appropriateness of a given suicide is the quality of the life that the suicide ends. If, when judged in the right way, the quality of a life is (or will soon fall) below the level that makes it worth continuing, then, all things being equal, suicide is not inappropriate. By contrast, if the quality of life is above that level, then, all things being equal, suicide is inappropriate. As is to be expected, however, there is much disagreement about when a life is worth continuing.

One kind of disagreement concerns the criteria for determining how good or poor the quality of a life is. An influential taxonomy[15] distinguishes three kinds of theory about the quality of a life: hedonistic theories, desire-fulfilment theories, and objective-list theories. According to hedonistic theories, the quality of a life is determined by the extent to which it is characterized by positive and negative mental states, such as pleasure and pain. Positive mental states enhance the quality of life, while negative ones diminish it. According to desire-fulfilment theories, the quality of life is determined by the extent to which a person's desires are fulfilled. The objects of one's desires might include positive mental states, but they also include various states of the (external) world. Finally, objective-list theories claim that the quality of a life depends on the extent to which it contains certain objective goods and bads. Having positive mental states and fulfilled desires must surely be included among the things that are objectively good for us. However, the objective-list view differs from the hedonistic and desire-fulfillment views in holding that some things make our lives better irrespective of whether they bring us pleasure or fulfill our desires. Similarly, on this view, other things diminish the quality of our lives irrespective of whether they cause pain or thwart our desires. Although objective-list theorists disagree among themselves about which things are objectively good and which are objectively bad, one can expect that there will be a lot of common ground. Some things could not reasonably be thought to be good, while others could not reasonably be thought to be bad.

Sometimes the differences between and within these three views will be irrelevant to whether a given life is worth continuing. This is because all the views agree that the given life either is or is not worth continuing. For example, a person who faces for the remainder of his life the choice of either unbearable pain or semi-consciousness is unlikely to be able to fulfill important desires, and his continued life is likely to be stripped of many important objective goods. However, the three views will not always converge in their judgments of a given life. In cases when their judgments diverge, it makes a difference which of the three views one adopts. I do not have the space here to adjudicate between the views. However, in any event, I would not want my qualified defense of suicide to depend on acceptance of one of the three views, for it would then have no effect on those who, notwithstanding any arguments I might advance for my preferred view, nonetheless hold one of its alternatives.

Determining the quality of a life, at least for the purposes of evaluating the suicide that ends it, is not merely a matter of establishing the extent to which the life satisfies a particular view's conditions for a good life. In the context of suicide, we need to consider not only how poor the quality of a life is, but also how poor the person whose life it is *thinks* it is. At one level, it is possible for the *actual* and *perceived* quality of a life to come apart. One can think that the quality of one's life is either better or worse than it really is.[16] There is another level, of course, at which the perceptions about the actual quality of a life constitute a feedback loop that affects how good the life actually is. Thus, if one thinks that one's terrible life is not that bad, then one's life is actually not as bad as it would be if one thought otherwise. Nevertheless, there is some value, as I shall show, in distinguishing between somebody's perception of his life's quality and how poor or good it actually is.

There is considerable variation in the quality of people's lives. How accurately people evaluate the quality of their lives also varies. Some people's assessments are less inaccurate than others. The possible relationships between lives of different qualities and peoples' perceptions of their lives' quality can be plotted on the set of axes in figure 7.1.

The worse the actual quality of somebody's life is, the lower on the vertical axis it should be placed. The worse a person's perceived quality of life is, the more to the left of the horizontal axis it should be placed. By combining both considerations, we may allocate somebody to any one of an indefinite number of positions in the area mapped out by the axes. The most accurate self-assessments of life's quality are to be found along the broken arrow, where people's self-assessments perfectly track the actual quality of their lives.

What bearing does this have on our assessments of suicide? First, the cases in which suicide is most appropriate are those toward the bottom of the broken arrow. These lives are of an

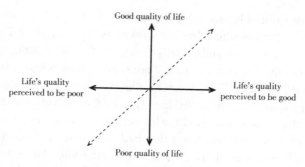

FIGURE 7.1 Actual and perceived quality of life.

appalling quality, and the people living them know them to be so. They want to die, and some of them do take their own lives. All those who think that suicide is sometimes permissible think that at least some of these suicides are among them. My earlier arguments responded to those people who think that suicide is wrong even for people living such wretched lives.

Second, and more interesting, is an important bias in most people's views about suicide. When discussing mistaken perceptions about the quality of life in the context of suicide, most people focus on those who underestimate the quality of their own lives. They focus on those, among the people to the left of the broken arrow, who contemplate, attempt, or successfully carry out suicide. The planned, attempted, or actual suicides of such people are deemed to be irrational because they are based on inaccurate assessments of the quality of their lives.

One reason why this focus is curious is that self-*under*estimates of life's quality are actually much less common than self-*over*estimates of the quality of one's life. As I noted in chapter 4, psychological research has shown, quite conclusively, that humans tend to have an exaggerated sense of their own well-being. Our self-assessments of our wellbeing are indeed unreliable, but almost always because we think that the quality of our lives is better than it really is, rather than because we think it is worse.

Recognizing the general human tendency toward overestimating life's quality is important for a few reasons. First, it calls into question whether those who are said to be underestimating the quality of their lives really are underestimating it. Although there probably are some people who truly do underestimate the level of their wellbeing, it is very likely that many of those who are thought by other people to do so are rather merely falling short of the normal exaggeration. If the norm is to have an inflated sense of how well one's life goes, then those who have either an accurate view of their wellbeing or merely a view that is less exaggerated than the norm will appear to most people as underestimating the quality of their lives.

The optimistic biases are so deeply ingrained in people (not least because of the evolutionary roots of these biases) that most people will simply deny that humans have them. However, that compounds a delusion with obstinacy. The evidence for an optimism bias is quite clear. Anybody who honestly wants to evaluate the reliability of self-assessments of quality of life must take this bias into account. Those who do recognize this bias will dismiss fewer self-evaluations of those people who judge their lives not to be worth continuing. Many of those who are pessimistic, depressed, or otherwise unhappy may actually have a much more accurate view of the quality of their lives than the cheery optimists who constitute the bulk of humanity.[17] The views of the unhappy may well be harder to have and to live with, but they may be more accurate and, in that sense, more rational.

Among the many people who overestimate the quality of their lives are some who, if they had a more accurate view, would carry out suicide (or at least consider or attempt it). Nothing I have said implies that it is irrational, all things considered, for these people to fail to kill themselves. Although their overestimation of the quality of their lives is a kind of irrationality, their perception of the quality of their lives, even if mistaken, is obviously relevant to an all-things-considered appraisal of their failure to kill themselves. First, the perception of one's quality of life affects the actual quality of one's life. A life that feels better than it really is, is actually better than it would be in the absence of that perception. This is not to say that the life is actually as good as it is perceived to be, but rather that the perception has a positive impact on the actual quality of life. Second, it obviously matters in itself how good or bad one's life feels, irrespective of its actual quality. If it feels worth continuing, then it is obviously not so burdensome as to make one prefer death, even if objectively one would be better off dead.

However, those reluctant to respect particular suicides should note that parallel claims can be made about those few cases in which people really do underestimate the quality of their lives. That perception does make their lives worse than they otherwise would be. If they feel that their lives are not worth continuing, then their lives have become so burdensome that they prefer death. Although their perception may be mistaken and thus irrational in this way, their preference for death may be rational in another way—given how burdensome the life feels, death may be best for this person.

Now it may be suggested that, notwithstanding these similarities, there is a crucial difference between cases when people overestimate and cases when people underestimate the quality of their lives. When somebody truly underestimates, we should try to convince him that his life is not as bad as he thinks it is, particularly if his being convinced would prevent his suicide. By contrast, in the case when somebody overestimates the quality of his life, we should not try to convince him that he is deluded and his life is actually not worth continuing.

There is indeed an important difference here, but we need to understand what accounts for it and the circumstances under which it may be eliminated. Consider first a person who seeks to kill himself because he truly underestimates the quality of his life. One important reason why we would try to show him that his life is actually better is that we would thereby bring him some relief.[18] By contrast, if we tried to convince the person who mistakenly overestimated the quality of his life, we would actually increase his suffering to the point, if we were sufficiently persuasive, where he could no longer bear it and thus kill himself. One might be willing to bear the extra burden in exchange for the truth about oneself, but it is quite another matter to insist that others make the same tradeoff. Thus, when we have these asymmetrical responses, it is not because those who overestimate are less mistaken than those who underestimate. Instead, it is because it would be wrong to add to the burdens of somebody else's life.

It is important to realize, however, that this will not always hold. If somebody's quality of life is actually sufficiently appalling, and his optimism is only making things worse for him, then it may well be appropriate for a sensitive confidant to intervene. There certainly are circumstances in which the short-term additional burden of a more sober view of one's condition, which could lead to one's death, does spare one a much greater burden in the future. A trusted friend or family member could, in such circumstances, be warranted in raising this. He might reassure the wretched person that nobody could reasonably hold his suicide against him. Given the taboos against suicide, such assurances may come as a relief.

In summary, then, both underestimates and overestimates of one's quality of life are rationally defective. Critics of suicide typically focus only on the rational defects of those who underestimate the quality of their lives. Yet overestimation is much more pervasive. Moreover, given this pervasiveness, there are many cases where, although people are thought to be underestimating the quality of their lives, they in fact are not underestimating. They are often more accurately appraising the quality of their lives than the majority of people around them. However, the rationality of suicide is not reducible to whether one is or is not accurately assessing how good one's life is. There is a difference between whether one's view of the quality of one's life is rational and whether, given one's perception, suicide is rational. The perception of one's life's quality is important, but it is not always decisive.

Does meaninglessness in life warrant suicide?

So far, my focus has been on suicide in response to the poor quality of life. Meaning and its absence, as I noted in chapter 4, may be part of the quality of life, but if they are, they are only one component of it. Whatever view one takes about the relationship between meaning in and quality of life, it is helpful, even if only heuristically, to consider suicide as a response specifically to meaninglessness in life. If meaning in life is entirely distinct from quality of life, then we need to know whether suicide is a reasonable response to meaninglessness. If, by contrast, it is a component of quality of life, then it is helpful to isolate this component in order to determine what contribution, if any, it makes to rendering suicide reasonable.

I argued in chapter 3 that all human lives are meaningless from the cosmic perspective. That fact is not a warrant for suicide. One reason for this, as I argued in chapter 5, is that death is bad (in some way) even when, all things considered, it is not bad. When it is not bad, all things considered, this is because death is necessary to avoid a fate worse than death itself. The absence of cosmic meaningfulness does not in itself seem to be a fate worse than death, not least because, even after death, one's life—and one's death—will remain utterly meaningless from the cosmic perspective. In other words, death does not relieve that problem.

Of course, the *feeling* that one's life is cosmically meaningless can have broader ramifications by spilling over and affecting other aspects of quality of life. It is possible, at least in principle, that somebody could be so miserable in response to life's cosmic meaninglessness that death would be less bad than continued life.

However, while taking one's own life would bring relief from the angst associated with the absence of cosmic meaning, it would not *actually* give one's life any cosmic meaning. Thus, ending one's life is not the only—or best—possible response to the feeling of meaninglessness. A preferable alternative would be to moderate one's subjective response to the fact of cosmic meaninglessness, at least with regard to suicide. Admittedly, such moderating will be harder for some than for others. There may be some who simply cannot escape the misery by any means other than death.

While this is possible, it seems unlikely unless other things were also true. If, for example, the quality of a person's life were (otherwise) relatively good (that is, relative to the human norm), then it is unlikely that thoughts of cosmic meaninglessness would make a person so miserable that death would be not bad, all things considered. Thus, it seems that angst about cosmic meaninglessness would not be sufficient to warrant suicide. One's life would have to be going especially badly for the existential angst to either tip the scales or overdetermine the case for suicide.

One factor that would contribute to how well one's life is otherwise is the feeling that one's life either does or does not have meaning from some or other terrestrial perspective. If, for example, one feels that one's life has sufficient terrestrial meaning, the felt absence of cosmic meaning is unlikely to make one want to end one's life—unless the quality of life is bad in other ways. Thus, those most likely to be so miserable because of the meaninglessness of their lives that suicide might bring them relief are those who feel that their lives lack even sufficient terrestrial meaning (and this lack is not compensated for by the presence of other goods that contribute to quality of life). This group of people can be divided into two:

1. Those whose lives actually contain sufficient terrestrial meaning even though they do not recognize it; and
2. Those whose negative perception about the absence of terrestrial meaning is veridical.

Given that death is bad, it seems as though it would be preferable for those in the first category to understand that, while their lives may be cosmically meaningless, they do have other kinds of meaning. Indeed, ending their own lives may well undermine what (terrestrial) meaning their lives do have. If your life is meaningful on account of the impact it has on your family or your community or even on humanity, then ending your life may actually attenuate that meaning. There are exceptions, of course, where one's terrestrial meaning actually lies in giving up one's life. In general, however, death undermines rather than enhances the terrestrial meaning of people's lives.

What about those in the second category—those who correctly appraise their lives to be devoid not only of cosmic meaning but also of terrestrial meaning? Is suicide a reasonable response to their situation? One consideration is whether they can infuse their lives with satisfactory terrestrial meaning. Cosmic meaning is beyond the reach of all. Terrestrial meaning is within the reach of most—but not all. Some people simply fail to create any meaning in their lives. They have no (positive) impact on anybody. If the rare people in such circumstances can change that, by making their existence valuable to some others, then they would come to have grounds for thinking that their lives have (some) terrestrial meaning. If, however, they are simply unable to create sufficient terrestrial meaning and their lives have no other redeeming features, then suicide many indeed be reasonable. Death would still be bad, but it might well be less bad than an utterly meaningless life of poor quality.

These thoughts can be graphically summarized in figure 7.2.

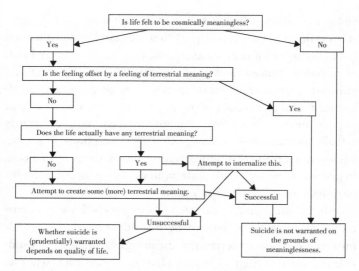

FIGURE 7.2 Meaninglessness and the warrant for suicide.

Restoring an individual's control

In coming into existence, we are guaranteed to suffer harms. The nature and magnitude of those harms vary from person to person. However, it is more common than not for these harms to include formidable ones: grinding poverty (and its associated costs), chronic pain, disability, disease, trauma, shame, loneliness, unhappiness, frailty, and decrepitude. Sometimes, these mark an entire life. Other times, they begin to intrude into a life that was previously devoid of them. For example, no matter how youthfully robust one may be now, a time will come when one will become enfeebled, unless something else gets one first.

Although there are some things we can do to prevent or delay some of these harms, our fate, to a considerable extent, is out of our control. We may attempt to preserve our health, but all we can do thereby is reduce, not eliminate, the risks. Therefore, we have some, but relatively little, control over whether these harms will befall us.

The degree to which we have control over whether our lives have terrestrial meaning varies, depending on whether the terrestrial meaning is more or less expansive. The more expansive the meaning, the less control we have. We have absolutely no control over the fact of our cosmic insignificance.

The only actions that could have guaranteed that we not suffer these fates are actions over which we had no control, namely, the actions that would have prevented us from coming into existence. These actions were within the control of our parents (and sometimes others), but never within our control.

Thus, we are involuntarily brought into a cosmically insignificant existence that bears considerable risk of serious harm. We did not and could not consent to our coming into existence. Nor can we ever wrest this control from those who exercised it. However, it is still possible to decide whether to terminate one's existence. That, of course, is a quite different sort of decision from a decision to bring somebody into being. When a person is not brought into existence, there is no cost for that person, for she never exists. Those who do not exist have no interest in coming into existence. By contrast, once one has come into existence, one typically has an interest in continuing to exist. Unlike never coming into existence, ceasing to exist is tragic. One reason it is tragic is that it involves the annihilation of the one who dies. In cases of rational suicide, it is also tragic because the interest in continued existence is outweighed by the interest in avoiding the burdens of life.[19] Thus, suicide should not be seen glibly, as it sometimes is, as a ready solution to a person's predicament. Nevertheless, suicide may sometimes be viewed as the least unattractive option.

If suicide were impermissible in all those cases in which competent people judged their lives to be not worth continuing, then those people would be trapped. Life would have been forced on them, and they would have to endure whatever life dished out. It is bad enough that prospective parents see fit to create people who, as a consequence, will suffer. It is worse still, once these people are created, to condemn a decision they might make to terminate their lives. To deny people the moral freedom to kill themselves is to deny them control over a decision of immense importance to them.

This argument has implications not only for the most noxious of conditions people may face, but also for conditions that, although significantly bad, are not the worst that life has to offer. First, although it may matter more to us that we not be trapped in lives whose quality is (or has dropped to) the lowest level, it also matters a great deal to many people that they not be trapped in lives that, although not this bad, are nonetheless very unpleasant. Second, because one would no longer have to endure any of the hardships of life if one ceased to exist, they are all avoidable.

We must keep in sight, of course, the fact that once we have come into existence, life's hardships are only avoidable at a cost. (Life's cosmic meaningless is unavoidable even by death.) Thus, if suicide is to be reasonable, the hardships need to be bad enough to offset that cost. Yet it is clear that these sorts of trade-offs are heavily dependent not only on how bad one's life actually is (or even on how bad one perceives it to be), but also on the amount of value that one attaches to life of a certain quality. There is a tendency to attach immense value to life itself and thus to favor it heavily in tradeoffs between death and continued life with an unfortunate condition. However, those who attach *relatively* less positive weight to life and relatively more negative weight to reductions in quality of life are not obviously unreasonable. Indeed, some might argue that this is more reasonable. They might say that it is very likely that the high value we attach to life is at least significantly influenced by a brute biological life drive, a strong instinct for self-preservation that is pre-rational, shared with other animals, and then, in the case of humans, rationalized. These biological origins of our valuing of life by no means show that life is not valuable, but recognizing the evolutionarily ancient, pre-rational grounds of the life drive does call into question any illusions we might have that the degree of value attached to life is exclusively the product of careful, rational deliberation. There is nothing unreasonable about the person who says that though he would rather continue living, that preference is not so strong that he would rather continue living in an unpleasant condition. Those with a lower tolerance for the burdens of life may think it would be stupid for them to persevere when the end of those burdens is achievable. Thus, it might be the case that we should be less averse to suicide (and death more generally) *not* because the Epicureans are correct that death is not bad, but rather because life is much worse than we think.

Conclusion

Suicides tend to shock. This is not merely because the deaths they bring about are often unexpected by those who hear of them. It is also because they run counter to the deep-seated, natural instinct for self-preservation. Humans, like other animals, will go to great lengths to delay their own deaths. They are usually willing to incur considerable hardship if that is the only alternative to death, even though, once dead, that hardship will be over and one will no longer exist to regret the loss of the extra life one would otherwise have had. How else can we explain the cancer patient who endures the harrowing effects of treatment for the extra months of life it affords her, or the concentration camp inmate who endures "excremental assault"[20]—the complete defilement and degradation, by means of excrement and other bodily effluvia—in order to survive the Holocaust?

Those who take their own lives, especially when the quality of those lives is much less bad than those of the cancer patient or the concentration camp prisoner, fly in the face of the normal will to live. They are seen as abnormal, not merely in the statistical sense of being unusual, but in the sense of being defective, either morally or psychologically.

I have argued that this response is inappropriate. Suicide is sometimes morally wrong, and it is sometimes the consequence of psychological problems. However, it is not always susceptible to such criticism. If we step back from our powerful survival instinct and our optimism bias, ending one's life may seem much wiser than continuing to live, particularly when the burdens of life are considerable. Moreover, it would be indecent to condemn those who, having deliberated carefully about the matter, decide that they no longer wish to endure the burdens of a life to which they never consented. They ought to take the interests of others, especially family and friends, into account. This is particularly true of those (such as spouses and children) to whom obligations have been voluntarily undertaken. The presence of such connections and obligations will trump lesser burdens, morally speaking. However, once the burdens of life reach a certain level of severity (determined, in part, by the relevant person's own assessment of his life's value and quality), it becomes indecent to expect him to remain alive for the benefit of others.[21]

8 | Conclusion

They give birth astride of a grave, the light gleams an instant, then it's night once more.

—SAMUEL BECKETT

Waiting for Godot: A Tragicomedy in Two Acts
(London: Faber and Faber, 1965 [1956]), 89

The human predicament in a nutshell

The human predicament has a number of interlocking features. First, human life, as is the case with all life, has utterly no meaning from the cosmic perspective. It is not part of a grand design and serves no greater purpose, but is instead a product of blind evolution. There are *explanations* of how our species arose, but there are no *reasons* for our existence. Humans evolved and, in time, the species will become extinct. The universe was indifferent to our coming, and it will be indifferent to our going. (Obviously, it will be indifferent not because it has attitudes and simply does not care about us, but because it has no attitudes at all.) All the great human achievements—the buildings, monuments, roads, machines, knowledge, arts—will crumble, erode, or vanish. Some remnants may remain, but only until the earth itself is destroyed. It will be as if we never were. This is true of the species and, a fortiori, of its individual members.

This does not imply that the lives of humans have *no* meaning. However, that meaning is severely limited. The only meaning human life can have is from some or other terrestrial perspective. The more expansive the meaning within this earthly realm, the harder it is to attain. Most of us make very small and local impacts. We shall be forgotten within a generation (or two) of our deaths, once those few on whom we have made an impact have also died.[1]

The extent to which one's life does or does not have meaning is, at least on some views, one measure of how well one's life is going. It is certainly not the only measure. There are other aspects that affect the quality of one's life. All things considered, the quality of human lives is not only much poorer than most people recognize it to be; it is actually quite bad. Just how bad it is varies from person to person. Some are unluckier than others, but even the relatively fortunate do not fare well, at least not in the long run. The claim is not that life is terrible at every moment. Instead, the claim is that life contains many serious risks and harms that are routinely overlooked, and that sooner or later within a person's life, the harms are likely to reach thoroughly indecent proportions. That some fates are entirely horrific—being burned alive, riddled with metastatic cancer, or losing all one's family—offers absolutely no protection against them befalling one. (There are things one can do to minimize bad outcomes, but the horror of them is not itself a guarantee that they will not occur, as the voluminous instances of horror graphically testify.)

Some might be inclined to respond that if life is so bad and so meaningless, then surely death should be welcome. However, that does not follow. First, the fact that we die is part of the reason that it matters that life lacks meaning. It is one fact that

gives rise to the yearning for meaning. If we were not temporally limited in this way, then meaning would be less important
to us. Our eternality would probably diminish, if not obviate,
the need to leave a mark or serve some purpose. Second, the
reason the human predicament really is a predicament is that
we are caught between a rock and a hard place. Life is bad, but
so is death.

Death is bad not only because of the future good of which it
deprives one, but also because it annihilates one. The upshot of
this is that even when death is not bad, all things considered—
because it does not deprive one of any good, or at least not of
enough good to outweigh the future bad—it is nonetheless very
bad because of the annihilation factor. The only time that death
is not bad at all is when one has been annihilated before (biological) death by, for example, being reduced to some advanced state
of dementia or a vegetative condition. In such circumstances, the
person is annihilated—or even dies in the psychological sense—
before he dies in the biological sense.

Because death is not the worst thing that can happen to somebody, claiming that death is bad does not imply that immortality
would be good, all things considered. There is no shortage of scenarios in which immortality would indeed be worse than dying.
But living forever is a very long time and thus, even if immortality were bad, it might nonetheless be bad that we do not live for
longer than the current human lifespan. Yet we should go further
and say that, under the appropriately specified conditions, the
option of immortality would indeed be good. This is, of course,
a merely theoretical consideration because mortality is so deeply
entrenched in the nature of reality that we could never actually be
immortal. Its mere unattainability, however, does not contradict

the claim that, under the right circumstances, it would be better than mortality.

There are two important things to say about suicide. First, because one feature of the human predicament is that there *are* fates worse than death, suicide must be an option. It is unconscionable for a person upon whom existence was thrust not to have the option to exit if continued existence becomes unbearable. Second, because death is bad, not only for the person who dies but also for loved ones who survive him or her, it is glib and callous to respond to the pessimist about the human condition by saying: "If it is so bad, just kill yourself!" Such responses simply fail to appreciate the predicament.

The human predicament is in fact an *in*human predicament because it is so appalling. It is inhuman primarily in a metaphorical sense because "inhuman" denotes cruelty, and cruelty presupposes agency. Yet the human predicament, writ large, is fundamentally and overwhelmingly not the product of any agent. It is the product of blind evolutionary forces that are indifferent to us.

Of course, once agency evolved, cruelty in a more literal sense exacerbated the human predicament. Humans inflict colossal quantities of suffering and death on other humans. The deceits, degradations, betrayals, exploitations, rapes, tortures, and murders, for example, aggravate the predicaments of individual humans. Another way in which agency plays some role in the human predicament is through procreation, the sexually transmitted "virus" that spreads existence and also spreads the existential predicament. This recreation of the predicament is not usually the product of cruelty. The usual causes are negligence and indifference in the case of those who reproduce without intending to do so, and selfishness or misplaced altruism in the case of those who do aim to create new humans.

Pessimism and optimism (again)

In the introduction, I said that I would describe any view that depicts some element of the human condition in negative terms as pessimistic, and any view that depicts some element of the human condition in positive terms as optimistic. That usage is neutral on the question of which view, in a given situation, is the more accurate. It does not make it true by definition that optimists have an *unduly* rosy picture or that pessimists have an *unduly* grim view of the world. A view is described as either optimistic or pessimistic depending on whether it is a rosy or a grim picture. It is then a separate question as to whether the view is an *excessively* rosy or grim one, or whether it is instead accurate.

Therefore, that a view is pessimistic should, in itself, neither count in its favor nor against it. (The same, of course, is true of an optimistic view.) Things are the way they are, and the best arguments support some evaluations rather than others. Insofar as things are good, they should be seen as such, and to the extent that they are bad, we should recognize them to be so. Pessimism is misguided when we have good reason to be optimistic, and optimism is misguided when we have good reason to be pessimistic. For example, a young person in good health and not in any special danger would usually be misguided in being pessimistic about his prospects for surviving to his next birthday. It is possible but unlikely that he will die before then. By contrast, the same young person would be rightly pessimistic about becoming a centenarian. It is possible but not likely that he will reach that age.

Thus, there can be no generalized defense of either optimism or pessimism. We should be optimistic about some matters and pessimistic about others. The human condition, I have argued, calls for a heavy dose of pessimism, although there is some limited scope for optimism. For example, although cosmic meaning is unattainable, it does not follow that nothing matters from any perspective. Some things matter even though they do not matter *sub specie aeternitatis*. One should not desist from loving one's family, caring for the sick, educating the young, bringing criminals to justice, or cleaning the kitchen merely because these undertakings do not matter from the perspective of the universe. They matter to particular people now. Without such undertakings, lives now and in the near future will be much worse than they would otherwise be.

We should have some optimism about the possibility of our lives having meaning from some limited terrestrial perspective, but that does not mean we should be optimistic about the bigger picture. We should not assume that our lives can have more meaning than they actually can have. Nor should we lull ourselves into the comforting thought that because more expansive meaning is unattainable, it would not be good to have such meaning.

Most people resist pessimistic views even when such views are appropriate. This is especially true with reference to a primarily pessimistic view about the human condition. The truth is simply too much for many people to bear. Thus, we find various attempts to bolster optimism and undercut pessimism, some subtle and some explicit.

First, few people like a grouch, which is why we have aphorisms such as "laugh and the world laughs with you, cry and you cry alone."[2] There is plenty of social pressure, often implicit, to put on a brave face and be cheerful.[3] Of course, not all pessimists appear to be grouchy, but the fact that pessimistic views are so often hidden from view only further reduces other people's exposure to them and makes those views seem more abnormal.

Second, pessimism is thought to be excessively negative and frequently even pathological. Sometimes, it is indeed either or both of these things, but not always. Sometimes, it is the optimistic view that is inaccurate, and the pessimistic one that is more accurate. That is exactly what I have argued with respect to the human condition. Moreover, optimism can also reach pathological proportions. Of course, there is some debate about what constitutes psychopathology, but if delusional states (no matter how widely they are shared) and maladaptive behavior are among the grounds for diagnosis, then "manic" optimistic states can sometimes fit the bill.

Third, pessimism has sometimes been dismissed as a "macho" attitude. The idea is that the pessimist is saying, "I am tough enough to see the facts,"[4] but "you optimists are weaklings." This charge is tendentious. Calling an attitude macho is pejorative because it implies bravado, rather than courage or mere intellectual honesty. Thus, the question is whether pessimism can plausibly be described as displaying bravado. I do not think it can. After all, pessimism bemoans the terrible human predicament and is sensitive to the vast amounts of suffering in the world. Using the word "macho" to describe the view of sensitive lamenters sounds like a clear misapplication of the word. The word seems much more suitably applied to a view that pretends everything is just fine (when it is not), and a fortiori when it is applied to those who think that pessimists should stop whining.

This does not mean that there are not pessimists with swagger. However, there are also optimists who have at least as much bravado as the most macho pessimists. Consider, for example, the following dedication in an edited collection on optimism and pessimism: "To my parents, who always have believed in me and who taught me that anything was possible as long as I worked hard enough."[5] The implication of this is that failure means that one did not work hard enough. The possibility that circumstances could conspire against one (and that there may be situations in which no matter how hard one works, one cannot achieve one's goals) is ignored by this sort of optimism,[6] which some might take to be bluster.[7]

Responding to the human predicament

How should one respond to the human predicament? One obvious response is to desist from perpetuating it by creating new humans who will inevitably be in the same predicament. Every birth is a death in waiting. When one hears of a birth, one must know that it is but a matter of time before that new human dies. Sandwiched between birth and death is a struggle for meaning and a desperate attempt to ward off life's suffering. This is why a pessimistic view about the human condition leads to the anti-natalist conclusion that we ought not to procreate.[8]

It is true that having and rearing children can help one cope with the human predicament. Children are one means to creating some terrestrial meaning. They can also enhance the quality of their parents', siblings', and others' lives. However, this is not a justification for procreating. The lesser reason for this is that there are other ways to create meaning and enhance the quality of one's life. The more important reason is that creating children in order to secure these goods constitutes participation in a procreative Ponzi scheme.[9] Each generation creates a new one in order to mitigate its own situation. Like all Ponzi schemes, this one will not end well. There will inevitably be a final generation. The earlier that generation is, the fewer people will be thrust into existence and thus into the human predicament.

The decision whether or not to procreate is only one part of a human life, and so we need to ask how *else* one should respond to the human predicament. One can avoid creating new people, but one already exists oneself. What should we do about the predicament in which we find ourselves?

Because the most drastic (and thus controversial) response is to take one's own life, I devoted a separate chapter to considering suicide. I offered a very qualified defense of this response. It is a— even *the*—rational response when the quality of life is so poor that life is not worth continuing, except in cases where the interests of others are sufficiently strong to override one's (all things considered) prudential interest in death. I denied that the absence of meaning *sub specie aeternitatis* provided reasonable grounds for ending one's life. The absence of *any*—even terrestrial—meaning is best addressed not by taking one's own life, but by attempting to invest one's life with some meaning. The inability to do so might well factor into the quality-of-life assessment that would be necessary for any contemplator of suicide.

However, suicide is not the only response. Indeed, suicide only responds to some aspects of the human predicament. It can address the poor quality of life by removing the burden of continued life in such a condition. It does not usually add meaning,[10] although it can bring relief from the *feeling* that one's life is meaningless. Most obviously, suicide does not solve the problem that death is bad (even when it is not bad, all things considered). Instead, it hastens that bad.

Thus, we need to consider other possible responses. Some are adopted without explicit recognition of them as responses, because they are adopted without conscious recognition of the human predicament. There may be a conscious recognition that pessimists *think* there is a human predicament, but the response consists of *denying* the predicament. Thus, a range of substantial optimisms is one kind of response to the human predicament. In the previous chapters, I considered these optimistic responses and argued why we should reject them.

Of course, my argument does presuppose that we should reject views that are untrue. In response to this assumption, it might be argued that there are excellent pragmatic reasons for accepting optimism even if the claims it makes are false. After all, optimism makes life so much easier. It helps one confront all the horror of the human predicament. It thus mitigates or palliates the predicament. If the more objective features of the human predicament are unavoidable, at least we should be sheltered from those subjective features—including the perception of the objective features—that are avoidable.

We need to think carefully about what this pragmatic argument involves. It is most effective when offered in defense of others' optimistic beliefs, because the beneficial effect is most marked if one truly believes the optimistic view, but anybody who advances the argument cannot entirely believe it because they know that the optimism is a kind of placebo. It might thus be thought to form the basis of an argument for rearing children in an optimistic worldview or for indulging those who already have such a worldview. However, as I noted in chapter 1, optimism is not an innocent anodyne. While it soothes the optimist, it can also have noxious effects on others.

These may be mitigated, but not entirely avoided, if the pragmatic argument is employed in defense of a kind of compartmentalized optimism. The optimist might say: "I recognize the human predicament. It is horrible, but I want to adopt an optimistic view to help me cope. I shall continue, at the back of my mind, to be aware of the predicament, but I can compartmentalize those thoughts—or at least try to."

This is a less unreasonable position because it seeks to face reality by recognizing the predicament while also seeking some relief. We might call this response "pragmatic optimism." The main concern with it is whether the compartmentalization can be effectively maintained. There are twin dangers. The one is that the recognition of the predicament will become so eclipsed by the optimism that the optimism will be unchecked and become more dangerous. If, for example, one loses sight of the human predicament, one might create more people. The contrasting danger is that if the pessimism is kept sufficiently in mind to avoid the risks of unchecked optimism, it will negate the positive effects of optimism.

Some may be able to steer the path between these perils. However, for capable navigators, there is another, preferable option. Instead of steering between optimism and pessimism, one can embrace the pessimistic view, but navigate its currents in one's life. It is possible to be an unequivocal pessimist but not dwell on these thoughts all the time. They may surface regularly, but it is possible to busy oneself with projects that create terrestrial meaning, enhance the quality of life (for oneself, other humans, and other animals), and "save" lives[11] (but not create them!).

This strategy, which I call pragmatic pessimism, also enables one to cope. Like pragmatic optimism, it also attempts to mitigate rather than exacerbate the human predicament. However, it is preferable to pragmatic optimism because it retains an unequivocal recognition of the predicament by not compartmentalizing it to coexist along with optimism. It allows for *distractions* from reality, but not *denials* of it. It makes one's life less bad than it would be if one allowed the predicament to overwhelm one to the point where one was perpetually gloomy and dysfunctional, although it is also compatible with moments or periods of despair, protest, or rage about being forced to accept the unacceptable.

Although I have described pragmatic optimism and pragmatic pessimism as two (distinct) responses to the human predicament, this is a simplifying taxonomy. For example, the distinction between a denial of reality and distractions from it is not a sharp one, not least because there are ambiguities in the word "denial." It can be used literally, but sometimes it is used more metaphorically to refer to what I have called distractions.[12] Thus, there is actually a wide range of responses along a spectrum from thoroughly deluded optimism to suicidal pessimism. In extremis, suicide may be the preferred option, but until then, I am recommending a response within the approximate terrain of pragmatic pessimism.

Some pessimists may think that the appropriate response to the human predicament is more extreme than the one I have recommended. They might argue that we should stare at our predicament head on and not distract ourselves from its horror. However, I see no reason why such a stance is required. Facing reality is a virtue, but not the only one. Imagine a person who has a terminal disease from which she is expected to die within a few months. It is good for that person to recognize that fact and reflect on it, but it would not be good if she were so devoted to confronting her imminent death that she refused to spend time with her family and friends because that would constitute a diversion from contemplation of her impending death. It would similarly be bad if one spent one's entire life reflecting on one's predicament. Indeed, it is hard to imagine how somebody so devoted could lead any kind of life. One would stop working and eating, which, after all, are (or can be) diversions.

In sketching out the various possible responses to the human predicament, recommending some and rejecting others, I am not oblivious to temperamental differences between people. Some people have naturally sunny personalities, and others are more prone to dark and depressing thoughts. It is very difficult for people to moderate their instinctive responses. One can advise the gloomy pessimist to distract himself for his own good, but it is certainly easier said than done. Similarly, one can offer any number of arguments to the optimist, but the disposition toward optimism might run so deep that his optimism is, if not incurable, then at least intractable.

In addition to the human predicament, individual humans have their own personal predicaments, some of which are worse than others: All things being equal, the poor and destitute are worse off than those who are economically more privileged; the sick are worse off than the healthy; the ugly are worse off than the attractive; and the gloomiest pessimists are worse off than others, including those pessimists who have the gift of managing the negative impact of pessimism on their lives.

If we take a cold, hard look at the human condition, we see an unpleasant picture. However, there are powerful biological drives against fully recognizing the awfulness of the human predicament that explain why so many people succeed in putting it out of their minds for much of the time. This is a mixed blessing. Ignorance is an existential analgesic, but those who do not sufficiently feel the weight of the human predicament are also vectors for its transmission to new generations.

NOTES

Preface

1. David Benatar, *Better Never to Have Been: The Harm of Coming into Existence* (Oxford, UK: Oxford University Press, 2006).

2. David Benatar and David Wasserman, *Debating Procreation* (New York: Oxford University Press, 2015). Note that the first half of this book, including chapter 3, is my work alone, and thus the views there should not also be attributed to David Wasserman, with whom I was debating the ethics of procreation.

Chapter 1

1. Or *when* it will occur. Stanislaw Lec famously said: "Optimists and pessimists differ only on the date of the end of the world." Stanislaw Lec, it should be noted, was remarkably successful in delaying his own demise. Sentenced to death for a second attempt to escape a German work camp during the Holocaust, he was taken to dig his own grave. He used the shovel to kill his guard and successfully escaped.

2. A pessimistic joke says that whereas some think the glass is half full and others think the glass is half empty, both are mistaken because the glass is in fact three-quarters empty. (A still-more-pessimistic version of the joke has the glass completely empty.)

3. James Branch Cabell, *The Silver Stallion* (London: Tandem, 1971), 105. This wording is not ideal because the referent of "this" is ambiguous between the fact that the optimist makes the claim he does and the content of the optimist's claim. A better wording would have been: "The optimist proclaims that we live in the best of all possible worlds; and the pessimist fears *that what the optimist says is true*."

4. See, for example, John Martin Fischer and Benjamin Mitchell-Yellin: "The pessimist's thought is that, given immortality, a deep boredom ensues ... life would become, as it were, deadly dull" ("Immortality and Boredom," *Journal of Ethics* 18 (2014): 363).

5. In aggregating the various aspects, they could be weighted by importance if their importance varied.

6. I am not speaking here of financial costs.

7. I say more about this in "The theistic gambit" in chapter 3.

8. It has been suggested to me that most people do care about animal suffering, but that the care is not activated in most people unless they are exposed to vivid images of animal suffering. Even if that is true, most people's concern for human suffering is significantly greater, and that is sufficient to make my point.

9. The following anecdote does *not* constitute an example of such excoriation. When Elizabeth Harman, who had written an article in response to *Better Never to Have Been*, told me in 2010 that she was pregnant, my response was muted. She then said that I would just have to be happy for her. I responded along the following lines: "I *am* happy for *you*. It is your expected child for whom I'm not happy." (I repeat this anecdote, with real names, because Elizabeth Harman has already recounted it publicly, at a conference, and thus I presume that she has no objection. I have heard others repeat the anecdote inaccurately, and so I set the record straight here.)

10. I have received a vast number of communications in this vein in response to *Better Never to Have Been*.

Chapter 2

1. I am reminded of the joke about Sherlock Holmes and Dr. Watson who were out camping. They awake in the middle of the night and have the following conversation:

SHERLOCK HOLMES: Dr. Watson, look up and tell me what you see.
DR. WATSON: I see the starry heavens above.
SHERLOCK HOLMES: And what do you deduce from that?

DR. WATSON: I deduce that we are small and insignificant beings in a vast cosmos.

SHERLOCK HOLMES: No, you fucking moron; somebody stole our tent!

2. Here I assume Saul Kripke's view about the necessity of origins; *Naming and Necessity* (Cambridge MA: Harvard University Press, 1972), 111–114, also accepted by Derek Parfit; *Reasons and Persons* (Oxford, UK: Clarendon Press, 1984), 351–352.

3. The life itself is often indicated by a mere dash between the date of birth and the date of demise.

4. Richard Taylor provides a similar example. His is of the ruins of a house; "The Meaning of Life," in *Good and Evil* (Amherst, NY: Prometheus Books, 2000), 328–329.

5. There will inevitably be details that are more complicated, but the matter about which people are chiefly concerned (*whether* their lives have meaning) becomes reasonably clear.

6. Some philosophers who once held this view subsequently changed their minds. See, for example, Philip L. Quinn, "The Meaning of Life According to Christianity," in *The Meaning of Life* (second edition), ed. E.D. Klemke (New York: Oxford University Press, 1999), 57; E.M. Adams, "The Meaning of Life," *International Journal for Philosophy of Religion* 51 (2002): 71.

7. *Oxford English Dictionary.*

8. Tatiana Zerjal et al., "The Genetic Legacy of the Mongols," *American Journal of Human Genetics* 72 (2003): 717–721.

9. Iddo Landau makes this sort of suggestion. He speaks about "a sufficiently high degree of worth or value" as a necessary condition for a meaningful life; "Immorality and the Meaning of Life," *Journal of Value Inquiry* 45 (2011): 312.

10. Susan Wolf is one who holds this view; "Happiness and Meaning: Two Aspects of the Good Life," *Social Philosophy and Policy* 14 (1997): 207–225.

11. Some people think that the generic use of "his" and other such pronouns to refer to people of both or indeterminate sex is sexist. For an argument

that it is not, see David Benatar, "Sexist Language: Alternatives to the Alternatives," *Public Affairs Quarterly* 19 (January 2005): 1–9.

12. Thomas Nagel, "The Absurd," in *Mortal Questions* (Cambridge, UK: Cambridge University Press, 1979), 13.

13. Ibid., 21.

14. Paul Edwards distinguishes between the "cosmic" and the "terrestrial" perspective. See his "The Meaning and Value of Life," in *The Meaning of Life* (second edition), ed. E.D. Klemke (New York: Oxford University Press, 1999), 143–144.

15. In principle, there are perspectives between those of the universe and those of humans. For example, one might speak of galaxy or planetary system perspectives. However, for human purposes, these are functionally indistinguishable from the perspective of the universe.

16. The term *sub specie aeternitatis* is fairly commonly used among philosophers. I have previously contrasted this with *sub specie humanitatis*; see *Life, Death and Meaning* (Lanham, MD: Rowman & Littlefield, 2004, 2010); *Better Never to Have Been* (Oxford, UK: Oxford University Press, 2006). I use the term *sub specie communitatis* here for the first time. Further subdivisions are possible, of course. Thus, we might refer to lives that are meaningful from the perspective of the family as having meaning *sub specie familiae.* (I am grateful to Gail Symington and Clive "Chuck" Chandler for advice on the correct forms of the Latin terms.)

17. One could distinguish between different timeframes for individual meaning. Thus, something might be meaningful to an individual for a short period of his or her life, or it might be meaningful throughout his or her life. Obviously, meaning for a shorter duration is even more limited than meaning for a longer duration, but I shall not dwell on this nuance.

18. Unfortunately, there is not a term that neatly complements the other three. I have resorted to *sub specie hominis* (the perspective of an individual human). *Sub specie cuiusque hominis* or *sub specie hominum singulorum* might have been more explicit, but they would certainly have been more tortuous.

19. Panpsychists may disagree with this, but I shall not argue against their position here.

20. The question itself might be incoherent, depending on exactly how one understands it, but we do not need to consider those complexities here. Even if it is coherent, it just happens not to be the source of existential anxiety.

21. Distinctions between subjectivist and objectivist accounts of meaning in life are common. There are subtle differences between them, and people are often imprecise in their definitions. I use the terms in the specific way I define them here.

22. Richard Taylor, *Good and Evil* (Amherst NY: Prometheus Books, 2000), 323.

23. Susan Wolf, "Happiness and Meaning: Two Aspects of the Good Life," *Social Philosophy and Policy* 14 (1997): 211; Susan Wolf, *Meaning in Life and Why it Matters* (Princeton, NJ: Princeton University Press, 2010), 9.

24. In chapter 7, where I discuss suicide, I consider objective and also subjective meaninglessness.

25. Or the environment, but I shall focus on animals here.

26. Remember here my point that we should not take the notion of "perspective" too literally.

27. The comparison between significance and what is worthy of mention in a history is to be found in Guy Kahane, "Our Cosmic Insignificance," *Nous* 48 (2014): 752.

Chapter 3

1. The same is true, of course, of humanity. Humanity is not an experiencing subject. However, humanity, unlike the cosmos, is at least in part an aggregation of experiencing subjects.

2. I ignore here the contribution of satellites and other debris to space and our moon.

3. A.J. Ayer, *The Meaning of Life* (London: South Place Ethical Society, 1988), 28.

4. Garrett Thomson, *On the Meaning of Life* (Belmont, CA: Wadsworth, 2002), 53–54.

5. Robert Nozick, "Philosophy and the Meaning of Life," in *Philosophical Explanations* (Cambridge, MA: Belknap, 1981), 586.

6. This sort of response might have appeal not only to theists but also to those atheists who believe that although our lives have no cosmic meaning, God, if he had existed, could have endowed such a meaning.

7. It has been suggested to me that the circularity could be avoided if altruism is "intrinsically good or meaningful." Given that "good" is not equivalent to "meaningful" and we are here interested in the latter, let us focus on that. The claim that altruism is intrinsically meaningful seems confused. To say that altruism is intrinsically meaningful is to say that it has an intrinsic point, purpose, or significance. But surely whatever meaning altruism has must be derived from what it does for the beneficiary of the altruism. What would be the intrinsic point, purpose, or significance of altruism if there were no beings who could be the beneficiaries (or practitioners) of it?

8. This is not to say that an eternal afterlife could not make life more meaningful. If it met all the necessary conditions—including preserving the "self" and having a desirable quality—it would constitute a valuable transcendence of a temporal limitation, thereby preserving at least some meaning from the ante-mortem life. However, the advantage of an afterlife would exist even if there were an afterlife but no God who was granting it. Moreover, even if an afterlife gave meaning to lives once they exist, it could not plausibly be seen to be the purpose of creating those lives in the first place.

9. Upton Sinclair, *I, Candidate for Governor: And How I Got Licked* (Berkeley, CA: University of California Press, 1994), 109.

10. Jenny Teichman makes this point in response to Thomas Nagel. She writes: "How can Tom Nagel know this? Can he just decree that this is so? In actuality he simply infers that life has no external meaning from the fact that he cannot think of such a meaning. But that is a *non sequitur*"; "Humanism and the Meaning of Life," *Ratio* 6 (December 1993): 157.

11. Ibid., 158.

12. These are beliefs of Scientology. See William W. Zellner, *Countercultures: A Sociological Analysis* (New York: St. Martin's Press, 1995), 108.

13. An analogue of theodicy, Kimdicy is "the vindication of Kim goodness in view of the existence of evil."

14. I am not claiming that life is appalling for *everybody* in these countries. There may be some—typically elites—for whom the quality of life is *comparably* better.

15. M.B. Santos, M.R. Clarke, and G.J. Pierce, "Assessing the Importance of Cephalopods in the Diets of Marine Mammals and Other Top Predators: Problems and Solutions," *Fisheries Research* 52 (2001): 121–139 (see 128).

16. Christopher McGowan, *The Raptor and the Lamb: Predators and Prey in the Living World* (New York: Henry Holt and Co., 1997), 34.

17. Archie Carr, *So Excellent a Fishe: A Natural History of Sea Turtles* (Gainesville, FL: University of Florida Press, 2011 [1967]), 78.

18. Christopher McGowan, *The Raptor and the Lamb: Predators and Prey in the Living World* (New York: Henry Holt and Co., 1997), 12–13.

19. Ibid., 77–78.

20. It is often noted that if predators did not consume their prey, the prey animal population would outstrip their environment's capacity to feed them and they would die slower deaths. However, an omnipotent, omniscient, and omnibenevolent deity could surely have found a less violent, suffering-laden solution to this problem. One possibility would be sterility when a population grows too large.

21. There are attempts to claim that human self-awareness is what makes it possible for human life to have meaning. For some discussion of this, see Thaddeus Metz, *Meaning in Life* (Oxford, UK: Oxford University Press, 2013), 40–41. However, even if this is so, the kinds of meaning must be terrestrial meaning. Human self-awareness, or human distinctiveness more generally, seems absolutely irrelevant to cosmic meaning (although they certainly are relevant to the *sense* of cosmic meaninglessness).

22. See, for example, William Lane Craig, "The Absurdity of Life without God," in *The Meaning of Life* (second edition), ed. E.D. Klemke (New York: Oxford University Press, 1999), 40–56.

23. For example, it is often said that, without God, there can be no moral values. However, there is a vast and convincing literature rejecting this suggestion.

24. Stephen Law, "The Meaning of Life," *Think* 11 (Spring 2012): 30.

25. Ibid.

26. Kurt Baier makes this point. He draws the distinction between causal and teleological explanations; "The Meaning of Life," in *The Meaning of Life* (second edition), ed. E.D. Klemke (New York: Oxford University Press, 1999), 104–105.

27. Kurt Baier makes this distinction too. Ibid., 105.

28. I say that this is not true of all of us, because many people—by some estimates, half of all people—were not intentionally created. Instead, they were the unintentional byproducts of sexual intercourse.

29. His summary of the argument is this: "We possess value, and, if we are alone, nothing else in the universe does. Therefore we are the only thing that has value, and, trivially, possess most value. We're therefore of immense cosmic significance"; Guy Kahane, "Our Cosmic Insignificance," *Nous* 48 (2014): 756.

30. Ibid.

31. Ibid., 757.

32. For example, he says that "it would be very hard . . . to find authors who sincerely deny that the prolonged agony and death of numerous innocent humans and other animals in no way matters—makes no difference to value" (756).

33. He does acknowledge that some "would insist that we should also add living things . . . even in the absence of sentience" (757), but he does not seem to be embracing that view.

34. Guy Kahane, "Our Cosmic Insignificance," 761.

35. Ibid., 749–750.

36. Ibid., 749.

37. Ibid., emphasis in original.

38. He does not use this language, but in defending the claim that we possess value, he makes claims such as the one cited above: "it would be very hard ... to find authors who sincerely deny that the prolonged agony and death of numerous innocent humans and other animals in no way matters—makes no difference to value" (756). These are comments about value rather than about what people ought to do, but in saying that the suffering and death of sentient beings matter, he seems to be saying that these beings matter.

39. The absence of this concern is attributable not least to the fact that we are not (currently) under threat from hostile or indifferent extraterrestrial moral agents.

40. This is also why I think we should reject Iddo Landau's clever but ultimately flawed distinction between (a) "perspective" and (b) "standards of meaningfulness"; "The Meaning of Life *sub specie aeternitatis*," *Australasian Journal of Philosophy* 89 (December 2011): 727–745. He argues that while our actions may be invisible from a cosmic *perspective*, it still matters—has *meaning*—that we engage in worthwhile pursuits. God or a hypothetical cosmic observer could evaluate an action as meaningful even though it had very little if any effect. This will not work, however, because what seems to be going on here is that God or the hypothetical cosmic observer is in fact adopting a more local perspective, even though Professor Landau is calling it a cosmic perspective. The mistake is to misunderstand what a cosmic perspective is. If, for example, an astronaut is in space, the family meaning he has does not thereby become cosmic. Similarly, just because God or a hypothetical observer is not on earth, it does not mean that the perspective he adopts of earthly matters is not an earthly one.

41. Perhaps it will be argued that although earth is teeming with life, humans are the only terrestrial species with sapient capacities. However, even if one thinks that this gives humans some special value, it is still the case that humans would have still greater terrestrial value if

they were the only sentient beings (or some of a much smaller number of sentient beings) on earth.

42. Guy Kahane, "Our Cosmic Insignificance," 761.

43. Thomas Nagel, "The Absurd," in *Mortal Questions* (Cambridge, UK: Cambridge University Press, 1979), 11.

44. Ibid., 12.

45. Ibid.

46. Kurt Baier advances a similar argument. He says that if life "can be worthwhile at all, then it can be so even though it be short. And if it is not worthwhile at all, then an eternity of it is simply a nightmare"; "The Meaning of Life," in *The Meaning of Life* (second edition), ed. E.D. Klemke (New York: Oxford University Press, 1999), 128.

47. Thomas Nagel, "The Absurd," in *Mortal Questions*, 12.

48. Robert Nozick, "Philosophy and the Meaning of Life," in *Philosophical Explanations* (Cambridge, MA: Belknap, 1981), 594.

49. See, for example, Thaddeus Metz, *Meaning in Life* (Oxford, UK: Oxford University Press, 2013). Such authors do not typically draw attention to the narrower focus by labeling it as such.

50. Peter Singer, *How Are We to Live?* (Amherst, NY: Prometheus Books, 1995), 218.

51. Ibid., 211.

52. See also Peter Singer, *Practical Ethics* (third edition) (Cambridge, UK: Cambridge University Press, 2011), 294.

53. Peter Singer, *How Are We to Live?* 217.

54. Christopher Belshaw, *10 Good Questions about Life and Death* (Malden, MA: Blackwell, 2005), 124. Rejecting other possible criteria, he employs the same kind of argument at 112–113.

55. Guy Kahane, "Our Cosmic Insignificance," 760.

56. Susan Wolf, "Happiness and Meaning: Two Aspects of the Good Life," *Social Philosophy and Policy* 14 (1997): 215.

57. Guy Kahane, "Our Cosmic Insignificance," 763.

58. Ibid., 764.

59. Ibid., 763. Guy Kahane recognizes that "such a verdict would be not only harsh, but also unfair," but he does not abandon it entirely.

60. Tim Oakley, "The Issue Is Meaninglessness," *Monist* 93 (2010): 110.

61. Thomas Joiner, *Why People Die by Suicide* (Cambridge, MA: Harvard University Press, 2005), esp. 117–136.

62. Dr. Frankl did not distinguish between meaning and perceived meaning, but it is clear that the meaning that keeps people going is perceived meaning.

63. Viktor Frankl, *Man's Search for Meaning* (third edition) (New York: Simon & Schuster, 1984), 109.

64. Ibid., 84. He repeats the words approvingly at 109.

65. Ibid., 104.

66. Thaddeus Metz, "The Meaning of Life," *Oxford Bibliographies Online*, *http://www.oxfordbibliographies.com/view/document/obo-9780195396577/obo-9780195396577-0070.xml* (accessed June 9, 2010).

67. This formulation is neutral between the regret being "rationally required" and its being "rationally permissible." The latter claim is less extensive but sufficient to justify those who are concerned about the absence of cosmic meaning.

68. Our absence actually would very likely have made a positive difference on earth. See David Benatar, "The Misanthropic Argument for Anti-Natalism," in *Permissible Progeny? The Morality of Procreation and Parenting*, eds. Sarah Hannan, Samantha Brennan, and Richard Vernon (New York: Oxford University Press, 2015), 34–64.

Chapter 4

1. I do not think that "survivors' guilt" is an exception because that is not so much a positive good as the evasion of something terrible. However, there may be some exceptions, which is why I have qualified the claim with the word "tend."

2. These findings are mentioned by David G. Myers and Ed Diener, "The Pursuit of Happiness," *Scientific American* (May 1996): 70–72. See also Angus Campbell, Philip E. Converse, and Willard L. Rodgers, *The Quality of American Life* (New York: Russell Sage Foundation, 1976), 25.

3. Frank M. Andrews and Stephen B. Withey, *Social Indicators of Well-Being: Americans' Perceptions of Life Quality* (New York: Plenum Press, 1976), 334.

4. This evidence is reviewed by Shelley Taylor and Jonathon Brown, "Illusion and Well-Being: A Social Psychological Perspective on Mental Health," *Psychological Bulletin* 103 (1988): 193–210.

5. I was previously under the impression that the evidence unequivocally supported the conclusion that positive experiences were recalled more than negative ones. However, I have subsequently learned that the findings are more complicated. Some indication of this is provided in the next note.

6. For example, it may be that negative experiences dominate immediately. However, at least in "non-dysphoric" people, they fade to a greater extent than positive experiences do, such that in the long run, there is greater recall of positive experiences. Greater recall of the positive is clearer when this affects self-image. See Shelley E. Taylor, *Positive Illusions: Creative Self-Deception and the Healthy Mind* (New York: Basic Books, 1989); Margaret W. Matlin and David J. Stang, *The Pollyanna Principle: Selectivity in Language, Memory, and Thought* (Cambridge, MA: Schenkman Pub. Co., 1978); W. Richard Walker, Rodney J. Vogl, and Charles P. Thompson, "Autobiographical Memory: Unpleasantness Fades Faster Than Pleasantness over Time," *Applied Cognitive Psychology* 11 (1997): 399–413; W. Richard Walker et al., "On the Emotions That Accompany Autobiographical Memories: Dysphoria Disrupts the Fading Affect Bias," *Cognition and Emotion* 17 (2003): 703–723; Roy Baumeister et al., "Bad Is Stronger Than Good," *Review of General Psychology* 5 (2001), esp. 344, 356.

7. Ronald Inglehart, *Cultural Shift in Advance Industrial Society* (Princeton, NJ: Princeton University Press, 1990), 241–246.

8. Ibid., 242.

9. Ibid., 246.

10. Perhaps it will be argued that adapting to one's paralysis does constitute an improvement in one's objective condition. Some might

respond to this objection by saying that it ignores the distinction between the objective condition—paralysis in this case—and how one subjectively reacts to the objective condition. However, one can reject the objection even if one concedes that a feedback loop is possible, such that one's subjective assessment can, to some extent, actually affect one's objective condition. More specifically, one can concede that the feedback loop leads to *some* improvement in one's objective condition, but as long as one remains paralyzed, one's objective condition is considerably worse than one's subjective assessment may recognize.

11. Richard A. Easterlin, "Explaining Happiness," *Proceedings of the National Academy of Sciences* 100 (September 16, 2003): 11176–11183.

12. See, for example, Joanne V. Wood, "What Is Social Comparison and How Should We Study It?" *Personality and Social Psychology Bulletin* 22 (1996): 520–537.

13. For more on this, see Jonathon D. Brown and Keith A. Dutton, "Truth and Consequences: The Costs and Benefits of Accurate Self-Knowledge," *Personality and Social Psychology Bulletin* 21 (1995): 1292.

14. One can soil oneself anywhere, and thus this qualification is necessary.

15. For a description of what this can feel like, see Patricia A Marshall, "Resilience and the Art of Living in Remission," in *Malignant: Medical Ethicists Confront Cancer*, ed. Rebecca Dresser (New York: Oxford University Press, 2012), 94.

16. Dan Ariely, *Predictably Irrational* (revised and expanded edition) (New York: Harper, 2009), xxiii–xxiv.

17. Tony Judt, *The Memory Chalet* (New York: Penguin Press, 2010), 15.

18. Ibid., 17.

19. Ibid.

20. Ibid., 20.

21. Arthur Frank, *At the Will of the Body* (Boston: Houghton Mifflin, 1991), 27.

22. Christopher Hitchens, *Mortality* (New York: Twelve, 2012), 67. Did he mean the small of his *neck*?

23. Ruth Rakoff, *When My World Was Small* (Toronto: Random House Canada, 2010), 99.

24. American Cancer Society, "Lifetime Risk of Developing or Dying from Cancer," http://www.cancer.org/cancer/cancerbasics/lifetime-probability-of-developing-or-dying-from-cancer (accessed October 2, 2013).

25. Cancer Research U.K., "Lifetime Risk of Cancer," http://www.cancer-researchuk.org/cancer-info/cancerstats/incidence/risk/statistics-on-the-risk-of-developing-cancer (accessed October 6, 2013).

26. "Older" is a relative term. There are many children, young adults, and middle-aged people who suffer from cancer, but septuagenarians, for example, are more likely to get cancer than children, young adults, and the middle-aged.

27. I say more about this in chapter 5.

28. Philip A. Pizzo, "Lessons in Pain Relief—A Personal Postgraduate Experience," *New England Journal of Medicine* 369 (September 19, 2013): 1093.

29. William Styron, *Darkness Visible: A Memoir of Madness* (New York: Random House, 1990), 47.

30. Ibid.

31. Ibid., 49.

32. Ibid., 62.

33. For more on this, see David Benatar, "The Misanthropic Argument for Anti-Natalism," in *Permissible Progeny? The Morality of Procreation and Parenting*, eds. Sarah Hannan, Samantha Brennan, and Richard Vernon (New York: Oxford University Press, 2015), 34–64.

34. One rape victim observes that "imagining what it is like to be a rape victim is no simple matter, since much of what a victim goes through is unimaginable"; Susan J. Brison, *Aftermath: Violence and the Remaking of a Self* (Princeton, NJ: Princeton University Press, 2002), 5.

35. Arthur Schopenhauer, "On the Sufferings of the World," in *Complete Essays of Schopenhauer* (Translated by T. Baily Saunders), Book 5 (New York: Wiley, 1942), 2.

36. However, even raising decent children requires plenty of hard work. There are so many ways of performing the task inadequately. The natural outcome of no parenting would be the adult into which a feral child grows, but any number of parenting mistakes can yield adults that approximate or are even worse than that outcome.

37. Some might argue that the achievements and greater wisdom of middle age outweigh the costs of decline by that stage. That is not implausible, but it would be even better if one had the benefits of middle age without the decline.

38. Henceforth, I shall not distinguish between desires and preferences as similar observations apply to both.

39. Abraham Maslow, *Motivation and Personality* (second edition) (New York: Harper & Row, 1970), xv.

40. Abba Eban is reputed to have said of an adversary that "his ignorance is encyclopedic." That insult is actually true of all of us. Abba Eban may have adapted it from an aphorism by Stanislaw Lec, who said, "Every now and then you meet a man whose ignorance is encyclopedic."

41. By "above a minimum quality threshold," I mean that the life is worth *continuing*. This is a lower quality threshold than that required for a life to be worth *beginning*. See *Better Never to Have Been*, 22–28.

42. Similar points can be made about moral goodness, aesthetic experience, and other capacities and traits.

43. Some might wish to sweep everything in this section ("Why there is more bad than good") aside by adopting some version of a subjective account of quality of life. For example, if one's life is as good as one thinks it is, and most people think that their lives have more good than bad, then most lives have more good than bad. One problem with such an account is that it allows no room for people to be mistaken. There are more sophisticated subjective accounts that attempt to address this shortcoming. For example, Wayne Sumner in *Welfare, Happiness, and Ethics* (Oxford, UK: Clarendon Press, 1996) has argued for an account that equates quality of life (or "welfare") with subjective life satisfaction on condition that the satisfaction is

both informed and autonomous. While not purporting to provide a sufficiently detailed response here, I can comment on the problem with this view. It fixes the required standards of "informed" and especially "autonomous" at a threshold that most adults of normal intelligence can meet. However, it is not clear to me why that should be the case. If there were a species that were as much more autonomous than us as we are than young children, they might well view the life satisfaction judgments of humans to fail the autonomy test (just as we think that young children fail the autonomy test). Indeed, they might point to the very psychological traits I have mentioned and cite these as evidence that humans are either ill-informed or do not autonomously process all relevant information in determining their life satisfaction. It might be unreasonable to override ordinary adults' decisions about how to lead their lives by appealing to hypothetical beings that are more autonomous, but it is quite a different matter to argue that ordinary adult humans' subjective life satisfaction judgments can be *fallible* even though they have species-normal levels of autonomy.

44. It should be noted that although religious faith can be optimistic, it is not always so. There are pessimistic religious views too.

45. Perhaps it will be suggested that these pains are byproducts of the instrumental value of pain in other contexts. If that is true, then our lives would be better if pain were present *only* when it had instrumental value (that is, if there were no spillover into cases where pain has no instrumental value).

46. In the case of the reflex arc, pain typically accompanies reflexive aversive behavior, but the pain plays no mediating role.

47. This is, of course, a variant of the stoical motto "no pain, no gain." Insofar as this motto is true, it is an unfortunate truth. (I am reminded here of the alternative motto for those less sanguine about pain: "no pain . . . no pain.")

48. Among those who have offered this version of the argument: Thaddeus Metz, "Are Lives Worth Creating?" *Philosophical Papers* 40 (July

2011): 252–253; David DeGrazia, "Is It Wrong to Impose the Harms of Human Life? A Reply to Benatar," *Theoretical Medicine and Bioethics* 31 (2010): 328–329.

49. It should be obvious that advocates of enhancement do not use the religious language I have included in scare quotes. I am using that language to highlight the parallels.

50. The qualification is important for the following reason: If human life is not worth creating in the absence of the enhancements, but the enhancements were of a sufficient magnitude to make life worth starting, it would be difficult to justify procreation if it would take a very long time for the enhancements to be brought about. The longer it takes to bring about the necessary enhancements, the longer people are creating lives that are not worth beginning.

51. Given the psychological phenomenon of comparison, such a life is likely to look much better to us than it actually is.

52. There are some transhumanists who claim that enhancements could lead to immortality. I discuss those claims in chapter 6.

Chapter 5

1. Benjamin Franklin, "Letter to Jean Baptiste Le Roy, 13 November 1879," in *The Writings of Benjamin Franklin*, ed. Albert Henry Smyth, Vol. X (New York: Macmillan, 1907), 69.

2. Letter to his brother, Jeremiah Brown, November 12, 1859; https://archive.org/stream/lifeandlettersof00sanbrich/lifeandlettersof00sanbrich_djvu.txt (accessed April 19, 2015).

3. If the meaning is to be positive, then one would have to add the condition that the soldiers whose lives are saved are fighting on the right side of a just war.

4. Epicurus, "Epicurus to Menoeceus," in *The Stoic and Epicurean Philosophers*, ed. Whitney J. Oates (New York: Random House, 1940), 30–31.

5. Epicurus uses the term "sensation," but the hedonistic position is more charitably presented if we speak not merely of sensations but of all

conscious states, including emotional ones. Thus, I shall use the term "feelings" to refer to the broader category of hedonistic states.

6. Thomas Nagel, "Death," in *Mortal Questions* (Cambridge, UK: Cambridge University Press, 1979), 5.

7. Some versions of these views are more discerning about which desires or preferences, if fulfilled, count as intrinsic goods. For example, they might say that only the fulfillment of "ideal" desires or preferences—those that one would have if one were fully informed and rational—are intrinsic goods.

8. Or at least that it is not irrational per se, for perhaps it is irrational to weigh continued life too heavily when balancing this good against the good of avoiding future suffering.

9. Those who think that prudential considerations are contingent upon one's future existence do so because they accept the existence requirement, which is a different way of interpreting the Epicurean argument. I shall consider this interpretation in the section entitled "When is death bad for the person who dies?" What I say there about the existence requirement's bearing on the deprivation account also applies to the existence requirement's bearing on the annihilation supplement.

10. Psychological connectedness refers to "the holding of particular direct psychological connections" between earlier and later times, and psychological continuity refers to "the holding of overlapping chains of strong connectedness"; Derek Parfit, *Reasons and Persons* (Oxford, UK: Oxford University Press, 1984), 206. Professor Parfit has defended the view that it is psychological connectedness and/or psychological continuity ("with the right kind of cause") that counts (215, 281–320). Although I have said that one can be concerned about one's annihilation even if what counts prudentially is psychological connectedness or continuity, Derek Parfit himself claims to care less about his death as a result (282).

11. Frances Kamm, *Morality, Mortality, Volume 1: Death and Whom to Save from it* (Oxford, UK: Oxford University Press, 1993), 43–53. Professor Kamm raises Limbo Man in support of her "extinction factor," which

has interesting similarities to my annihilation account. (I learned of this after writing the first draft of this chapter, and thus her extinction factor was not an influence on my annihilation account.)

12. Frances Kamm, *Morality, Mortality, Volume 1: Death and Whom to Save from it* (Oxford, UK: Oxford University Press, 1993), 19.

13. It might be suggested that if it is bad to destroy something of value, then it is also good to create something of value. Thus, just as the creation of great works of art is good, so creating new people is good. However, this does not follow. The reasons are complex, but one reason is that the notion of intrinsic value is often oversimplified. Some people think, mistakenly, that if something of a certain kind has intrinsic value, then creating more such things of that kind is good because it adds value to the world. However, it is possible to think that a person, for example, has intrinsic value (once created) without thinking that the prospective intrinsic value provides a reason for creating the person. To help see this, consider the (related) notion of moral considerability. One can think that sentient beings have value in the sense of being morally considerable without thinking that creating more morally considerable beings is good.

14. The implication here is that, on the deprivation account, death is not bad if it does not deprive one of any good. In response to this, it has been suggested to me that a deprivationist could still argue that the *conjunction* of the death *and* the condition that eliminated the possibility of further good is bad for the person who dies. However, all the work in that conjunction is being done by the condition that eliminates the possibility of future good. It is that condition that deprives. Once that condition has done all the depriving there is to do, death adds no further deprivation.

15. I recognize that our mourning practices might not perfectly track what is bad. Nonetheless, there are insights to be found. All things being equal, it should count in favor of an account of death's badness that it is more consistent with the parameters of reasonable mourning than other accounts.

16. I am grateful to Frances Kamm for this suggestion.

17. Jeff McMahan, "Death and the Value of Life," *Ethics* 99 (October 1988): 33.

18. By "non-experiential goods," I do not mean that they cannot be or never are experienced, but only that experiencing the goods is not necessary for counting them as goods.

19. This does not preclude the possibility that it is more bad at some times (perhaps immediately after the break when the pain is worst) than it is at others (such as just before the cast is removed).

20. The terms I use to describe the subsequent positions are used by a number of writers, although there are some taxonomic differences between them. See, for example, Steven Luper, "Death," in *Stanford Encyclopedia of Philosophy* (revised version), http://plato.stanford. edu/entries/death/ (accessed January 21, 2014); Ben Bradley, *Well-Being and Death* (New York: Oxford University Press, 2009), 84; Jens Johansson, "When Do We Incur Mortal Harm?" in *The Cambridge Companion to Life and Death*, ed. Steven Luper (New York: Cambridge University Press, 2014), 149–164.

21. Among the advocates of this view are George Pitcher ("The Misfortunes of the Dead," *American Philosophical Quarterly* 21 (April 1984): 183–188); and, following him, Joel Feinberg, *Harm to Others* (New York: Oxford University Press, 1984), 89–91.

22. One exponent of this view is Fred Feldman, *Confrontations with the Reaper: A Philosophical Study on the Nature and Value of Death* (New York: Oxford University Press, 1992), 153–154.

23. Ibid., 154; Fred Feldman speaks about Lindsay, his deceased daughter, rather than about Beth.

24. If it were not worth living, then according to the deprivation account, death would not be bad (all things considered).

25. Julian Lamont raises this concern. See his "A Solution to the Puzzle of When Death Harms Its Victims," *Australasian Journal of Philosophy* 76 (1998): 198–212. Steven Luper, drawing on Dr. Lamont, makes the point more clearly. See his "Death," *Stanford Encyclopedia of Philosophy*

(revised version), http://plato.stanford.edu/entries/death/ (accessed January 21, 2014).

26. Julian Lamont, "A Solution to the Puzzle of When Death Harms Its Victims," *Australasian Journal of Philosophy* 76 (1998): 198–212.

27. Thomas Nagel, "Death," in *Moral Questions*, 5.

28. Ibid.

29. Ibid., 6.

30. I add this qualification because some people may think that unless determinism is true, future events cannot have a truth value until they occur. Others, however, think that even if the future is not fixed, it is always the case that what will in fact happen will happen, even though what happens was not determined and could not have been known in advance.

31. I say "according to some views" because some might deny that it can be true until the truth-making conditions actually occur.

32. By "clever" people, I mean those who demonstrate a certain facility with the technicality of arguments and are clearly intelligent, but who display a lack of wisdom. For more on this, see David Benatar, "Forsaking Wisdom," *The Philosophers' Magazine* (First Quarter 2016): 23–24.

33. Posthumous bads share this feature with death.

34. Frederik Kaufman, "Pre-Vital and Post-Mortem Non-Existence," *American Philosophical Quarterly* 36 (January 1999): 1–19.

35. Derek Parfit makes this observation, although he thinks it would be better if we did not have this bias. Derek Parfit, *Reasons and Persons* (Oxford, UK: Oxford University Press, 1984), 170–181.

36. Fred Feldman, *Confrontations with the Reaper* (New York: Oxford University Press, 1992), 155.

37. Frederik Kaufman, "Pre-Vital and Post-Mortem Non-Existence," *American Philosophical Quarterly* 36 (January 1999): 11. In what follows, I outline Professor Kaufman's compelling argument.

38. Ibid.

39. Ibid., 3.

40. David Benatar, *Better Never to Have Been: The Harm of Coming into Existence* (Oxford, UK: Oxford University Press, 2006).

41. Shelly Kagan has suggested to me that the annihilation factor does not avoid the symmetry problem. Drawing on his distinction in *Death* (New Haven, CT: Yale University Press, 2012, 227) between "loss" (no longer having what one once had) and "schmoss" (not yet having what one will still have), he suggested that annihilation (ceasing to be) has a symmetrical parallel, which, as I recall, he dubbed "prehilation," but which I propose we might better designate as "exnihilation" (coming to be or perhaps ceasing not to be). Here is how he puts the objection in terms of "loss" and "schmoss":

   During the period after death there's a loss of life but no schmoss of life. And during the period before birth, there's no loss of life, but there is a schmoss of life. And now, as philosophers, we need to ask: why do we care more about *loss* of life than about *schmoss* of life? What is it about the fact that we don't have something that we used to have, that makes this worse than not having something that we're going to have? (227)

   I presume that applying this idea to exnihilation and annihilation, the final question in the quoted paragraph would be something like: "What is it about the fact that we will cease to exist (annihilation) that makes this worse than having come into existence (exhnihilation)? However, this question has a good answer, as I have suggested. It is that while we had no interest in coming into existence, we do have an interest in not ceasing to exist. (The asymmetry between exnihilation and annihilation is even stronger if one agrees with me that not only do we have no interest in coming into existence, but we also have an interest in *not* coming into existence.)

42. For more on different senses of interest, see David Benatar, *Better Never to Have Been*, 135–152.

43. Notice that this is a claim about death and not a more controversial one about euthanasia.

44. Some might suggest that coming into existence is also the enabling condition for all good things, but the bads and the goods are not symmetrical. See David Benatar, *Better Never to Have Been*, 30–40; David Benatar and David Wasserman, *Debating Procreation* (New York: Oxford University Press, 2015), 21–34, 37–38, 48–52. However, even if one rejects these arguments, see the asymmetry discussed in the next paragraph.

45. For a discussion of the evidence that sentience emerges late in gestation, see David Benatar and Michael Benatar, "A Pain in the Fetus: Toward Ending Confusion about Fetal Pain," *Bioethics* 15 (2001): 57–76.

46. Jeff McMahan, *The Ethics of Killing* (New York: Oxford University Press, 2002), 170.

47. Ibid.

48. The annihilation account and the time-relative interests account are not mutually exclusive. Thus, I am not arguing for the rejection of the time-relative interests account. Instead, my argument is that the annihilation account is an equally effective way of reaching the same plausible conclusions.

49. Jeff McMahan, *The Ethics of Killing*, 118.

50. Ibid. However, Jeff McMahan first used this example in "Death and the Value of Life," *Ethics* 99 (October 1988): 45.

51. Fred Feldman, "Some Puzzles about the Evil of Death," *Philosophical Review* 100 (1991): 225.

52. Jeff McMahan, *The Ethics of Killing* (New York: Oxford University Press, 2002), 120.

53. Ibid.

54. In chapter 6, I consider whether immortality would necessarily be bad.

55. Delaying it for a few seconds makes only a negligible or no difference.

56. The absurdity of this idea is highlighted by the following:

> In my next life I want to live my life backwards. You start out dead and get that out of the way. Then you wake up in an old people's home feeling better every day. You get kicked out for being too healthy, go collect your pension, and then when you

start work, you get a gold watch and a party on your first day. You work for 40 years until you're young enough to enjoy your retirement. You party, drink alcohol, and are generally promiscuous, then you are ready for high school. You then go to primary school, you become a kid, you play. You have no responsibilities, you become a baby until you are born. And then you spend your last 9 months floating in luxurious spa-like conditions with central heating and room service on tap, larger quarters every day and then Voila! You finish off as an orgasm!

This is often attributed to Woody Allen, George Carlin, or Andy Rooney, but Snopes.com suggests that a version of it is the work of Sean Morey. See http://www.snopes.com/politics/soapbox/rooney3.asp (accessed September 1, 2015).

57. Or death in the absence of annihilation—the view of those who think that we survive our deaths.

58. It does not matter whether the pre-death annihilation is gradual (as it is in the case of dementia) or whether it is instantaneous (as in the case of a stroke that reduces one to irreversible unconsciousness).

59. Strictly speaking, this is not an *atheist* T-shirt but an afterlife-denying T-shirt. One does not have to be an atheist to deny the existence of an afterlife. (I learned of this T-shirt when saw I Herb Silverman wearing it.)

60. Shelly Kagan, *Death* (New Haven, CT: Yale University Press, 2012), 292.

61. Benzion Netanyahu, who died in 2012, was predeceased by one of his sons, Yonatan, who was killed at age thirty while he led the assault unit in Israel's 1976 raid on Entebbe Airport to free hostages being held there. This is thus a dramatic example of the Grim Reaper's snipers picking out those whose "turn" has not yet come. The son dies at thirty, and the father lives to 102.

62. I am reminded here of the wealthy ninety-year-old, whose investment adviser says: "Have I got a great investment for you. I can double your money in five years." To this, his client responds: "Look, at my age, I don't buy green bananas!"

63. This is not to deny those cases in which the young have good reason to think that very little life remains.

Chapter 6

1. This particular term is Gerald Gruman's. See his *A History of Ideas About the Prolongation of Life* (New York: Springer Pub. Co., 2013), 3–5. He distinguishes "radical" from "moderate" prolongevitism. The former is the relevant category here as they aim at "the attainment of virtual immortality and eternal youth."

2. "As humans and computers merge . . . immortality?" *PBS NewsHour*, June 10, 2012. Transcript available here: http://www.pbs.org/newshour/bb/business-july-dec12-immortal_07-10/ (accessed January 4, 2015).

3. Ibid. This projection sets the outer date for this development at 2027. This is at odds with the projection that Ray Kurzweil and Terry Grossman reported (without disagreement) that "many experts believe" that "within a decade [of 2004] . . . your remaining life expectancy will move further into the future"; Ray Kurzweil and Terry Grossman, *Fantastic Voyage: Life Long Enough to Live Forever* (London: Rodale International Ltd, 2005), 4. (The book's copyright date is 2004.)

4. John Rennie, "The Immortal Ambitions of Ray Kurzweil: A Review of Transcendent Man," *Scientific American* (February 5, 2011), http://www.scientificamerican.com/article/the-immortal-ambitions-of-ray-kurzweil/ (accessed January 4, 2015).

5. He is quoted as saying this by Jonathan Weiner, *Long for This World* (New York: HarperCollins, 2010), 167.

6. Aubrey de Grey and Michael Rae, *Ending Aging: The Rejuvenation Breakthroughs That Could Reverse Human Aging in Our Lifetime* (New York: St. Martin's Griffin, 2007), emphasis mine.

7. Aubrey de Grey, "Extrapolaholics Anonymous: Why Demographers' Rejections of a Huge Rise in Cohort Life Expectancy in This Century Are Overconfident," *Annals of the New York Academy of Sciences* 1067 (2006): 88.

8. Ibid., 91.

9. For a detailed discussion, see Gerald Gruman, *A History of Ideas About the Prolongation of Life* (New York: Springer, 2013). For a briefer summary, see Steven Shapin and Christopher Martyn, "How to Live Forever: Lessons of History," *British Medical Journal* 321 (December 23–30, 2000): 1580–1582.

10. R.C. Merkle, an advocate of cryopreservation, concedes that "the process of freezing inflicts a level of damage which cannot be reversed by current medical technology," but he claims that the damage is likely to be reversible at some point in the future"; R.C. Merkle, "The Technical Feasibility of Cryonics," *Medical Hypotheses* 39 (1992): 6, 14.

11. "Cryonic Myths," Alcor Life Extension Foundation, http://www.alcor.org/cryomyths.html#myth2 (accessed January 4, 2014).

12. Cryopreservationists deny that that those preserved are dead, and thus they would resist the term "resurrection" if this is understood as literally bringing somebody back from death. However, "resurrection" need not be understood in this way.

13. The distinction is Stephen Cave's; *Immortality: The Quest to Live Forever and How It Drives Civilization* (New York: Crown Publishers, 2012), 63, 267. It is also employed by John Martin Fischer and Benjamin Mitchell-Yellin, "Immortality and Boredom," *Journal of Ethics* 18 (2014): 353–372.

14. Raymond Kurzweil and Terry Grossman, *Fantastic Voyage: Live Long Enough to Live Forever* (London: Rodale International Ltd, 2005), 272.

15. Eric Lax, *On Being Funny: Woody Allen and Comedy* (New York: Charter House, 1975), 232.

16. Jonathan Swift, "A Voyage to Laputa," Chapter X, in *Gulliver's Travels and Other Writings*, ed. Ricardo Quintana (New York: Modern Library, 1958), 165–172.

17. This, at least, was my understanding of the traditional (Jewish) view. The biblical text itself may seem to suggest otherwise, for Genesis 3:22–24 has God providing the fact that Adam and Eve might next partake

of the fruit of the tree of life and live forever as a reason for their ban-ishment of from the Garden of Eden. However, David M. Goldenberg (in a personal communication) has confirmed my interpretation of the traditional view, citing a number of sources, including Genesis 3:19 as well as Shabbat 55b and Eruvin 18b in the Babylonian Talmud. He understands Genesis 2:22 as indicating that eating of the fruit of the tree of life "would reverse the introduction of death."

18. Bernard Williams, "The Makropulos Case: Reflections on the Tedium of Immortality," in *Problems of the Self* (Cambridge, UK: Cambridge University Press, 1973), 82–100. Although this paper has been much discussed and admired, Bernard Williams's style of writing is not as plain as it could (and should) be.

19. Ibid., 91.

20. Ibid., 92.

21. John Martin Fischer, "Why Immortality Is Not So Bad," *International Journal of Philosophical Studies* 2 (1994): 261.

22. Bernard Williams, "The Makropulos Case: Reflections on the Tedium of Immortality," 89–91.

23. Ibid., 90, emphasis mine.

24. John Martin Fischer, "Why Immortality Is Not So Bad," 262–266.

25. Ibid., 263.

26. Ibid., 261, 266.

27. Roy Perrett, "Regarding Immortality," *Religious Studies* 22 (1986): 226; John Martin Fischer, "Why Immortality Is Not So Bad," 267. The examples John Martin Fischer provides are within adult life, whereas the example I now provide is arguably even starker. It is the difference between childhood and adulthood.

28. This is contrary to Geoffrey Scarre's concern. See his *Death* (Stocksfield, UK: Acumen, 2007), 58.

29. Bernard Williams, "The Makropulos Case: Reflections on the Tedium of Immortality," 82, 89.

30. Geoffrey Scarre, *Death* (Stocksfield, UK: Acumen, 2007), 58.

31. Ibid., 58–59.

Chapter 7

1. The human predicament is not a fate avoidable by death, but it is avoidable by *birth* (when "birth" is used loosely to refer to coming into existence).

2. I prefer the expression "a life not worth continuing" to "a life not worth living." This is because the latter expression is ambiguous between my preferred expression and "a life worth starting." This distinction is important because different standards should be used to evaluate lives that have already begun and those that have not. For more on this, see *Better Never to Have Been* (Oxford, UK: Oxford University Press, 2006), 22–28.

3. There are some exceptions. See, for example: Margaret Pabst Battin, *Ethical Issues in Suicide* (Upper Saddle River, NJ: Prentice-Hall, 1995); Valerie Gray Hardcastle and Rosalyn Walker, "Supporting Irrational Suicide," *Bioethics* 16 (2002): 425–438.

4. Suicide is no longer illegal in Western societies. However, *assisted* suicide remains illegal in all but a few jurisdictions. I have argued elsewhere for the legalization of assisted suicide and voluntary active euthanasia. See David Benatar, "Assisted Suicide, Voluntary Euthanasia, and the Right to Life," in *The Right to Life and the Value of Life: Orientations in Law, Politics and Ethics*, ed. Jon Yorke (Farnham, UK: Ashgate, 2010), 291–310.

5. R.G. Frey, "Did Socrates Commit Suicide?" *Philosophy* 53 (1978): 106–108.

6. A variant on this explanation is that murder is wrong because it thwarts the interests of the victim *or* violates their right to life. This version differs from the other one in delinking the right from the interest. Instead of viewing the right as protecting the interest, it views the right and the interest as distinct.

7. For example, I waive my right to claim a debt from you and thereby lose any future claim. However, notice that this sort of rights-waiving involves a right *in personam* rather than *in rem*.

8. Suicide has one advantage over voluntary euthanasia. Because the suicide kills himself, the rest of us have an extra level of assurance that he really wanted to die. This is because it probably takes greater conviction to perform the act oneself than to ask others to do it.

9. Other rights work in the same way. For example, a right to the confidentiality of some specified information may be waived with regard to a particular person if one allows one's doctor (but not anybody else) to share that information with a particular person. That is quite different from alienating one's right to confidentiality, which would allow anybody to convey any information to anyone else.

10. Many people, even today, lack access to palliative medicines.

11. David Hume offers this argument. See his "Of Suicide," in David Hume, *Essays: Moral, Political and Literary* (revised edition), ed. Eugene F. Miller (Indianapolis, IN: Liberty Classics, 1987), 583.

12. Although somebody who was successful in taking his own life was himself beyond the reach of punitive repercussions, neither his remains nor his estate were. Those who unsuccessfully attempted suicide were obviously more vulnerable.

13. It has been suggested to me that one situation in which the state's interest might be sufficiently strong to render suicide wrong would be when a person takes his own life in order to avoid the consequences of having done something very wrong, such as having embezzled large sums of money. Suicide would then be a way to avoid facing justice. However, I am not convinced that the state's interest would render suicide wrong in such cases, for the wrongdoer would have paid the price of his life—a much higher price than any just society would extract for even more serious wrongs. If the wrongdoer's suicide avoided not punishment but rather compensation to his victims—here we have to stipulate that his estate is insufficient to pay compensation, but through continued life, he could have generated income to pay restitution—then this could be a wrongful case of suicide. (Such cases would not always be ones in which the *state's* interests were those that made the suicide wrong.)

14. Although these duties may be taken over by others, sometimes this involves some setback to those who had a special relationship with the person who took his own life.

15. Derek Parfit, *Reasons and Persons*, 493–502.

16. Now it might be thought that whereas a person's perception of his life's quality could differ from the actual quality of his life on objective-list and even desire-fulfilment theories, the same is not possible on the hedonistic view. This is an error. One can be mistaken about how much pleasure and pain one's life actually contains. That one cannot be mistaken about whether one is currently having a pleasurable or a painful experience does not mean that one cannot be mistaken about how much pleasure and pain one has experienced so far or will experience in the future.

17. I am not here asserting that there is a generalized phenomenon of "depressive realism," about which there is conflicting evidence. Instead, I am making the more restricted claim that many pessimists have a more accurate subjective assessment of quality of life than optimists do. Indeed, one point of chapter 4 was to argue that the quality of human life is much worse than most people think.

18. We would also benefit those whose friends and family would be left behind if he killed himself, but my focus for the moment is on the interests of the prospective suicide himself.

19. Others might say that it is tragic because the burdens of life have become so great that one's interest in continuing to exist has been obliterated.

20. "Excremental assault" is Terrence Des Pres's term. It refers to one component of the treatment to which Nazi concentration camp inmates (and those in transit to such camps) were subjected. See his "Excremental Assault," in *Holocaust: Religious and Philosophical Perspectives*, eds. John K. Roth and Michael Berenbaum (New York: Paragon House, 1989), 203–220.

21. This chapter is adapted from David Benatar, "Suicide: A Qualified Defense," in *The Metaphysics and Ethics of Death: New Essays*, ed. James Stacey Taylor (New York: Oxford University Press, 2013), 222–244.

Chapter 8

1. Many leave "blind traces" for a longer period. For example, their genetic material will survive in their descendants, even though those descendants are unlikely to even know their identities beyond the third generation. It is thus not clear what value these somewhat more enduring impacts have. In any event, this impact will also last only so long.

2. A horoscope from *The Onion* reads: "Smile, and the world smiles with you; cry and you cry alone. But if you are standing over a pile of dismembered infants and there are TV cameras around, you should probably try for the opposite"; *Onion Calendar*, July 6, 2015.

3. For an extensive discussion of this, see Barbara Ehrenreich, *Bright-Sided: How the Relentless Promotion of Positive Thinking Has Undermined America* (New York: Henry Holt & Co., 2009).

4. Susan Neiman ("On Morality in the 21st Century," *Philosophy Bites* interview) said:

   Pessimism is an attitude that may look brave.... There are certain people who propose it with a rather macho stance ... [they say] "I'm tough enough to see the facts," but it is actually a very cowardly way of dealing with the world because if you only think that things can get worse ... then there is nothing to do but lie back in your armchair and shake your head at it, whereas if you think that there is some chance that human action could make the world just slightly better or even keep it from getting worse ... you're actually responsible then for doing some small bit of something in your own lifetime. So the idea that pessimism is somehow brave or honest is ... a sleight of hand.

   Her subject was pessimism about social progress. Nevertheless, it seems that if the imputation of toughness is appropriate in that case, it could not be withheld in the case of pessimism about the existential questions covered in this book.

5. Edward Chang (ed.), *Optimism and Pessimism: Implications for Theory, Research and Practice* (Washington, DC: American Psychological Association, 2001).

6. It would be cruel to wish that the optimists' faith be tested, but it would be nice if optimists could test pessimists' faith by being as nice as they can be to them.

7. I am not suggesting that parents should impart the fatalistic view that one's attitude never makes a difference. However, there are lessons intermediate between fatalism and unreasonable optimism.

8. For other arguments for anti-natalism, see David Benatar, *Better Never to Have Been: The Harm of Coming into Existence* (Oxford, UK: Oxford University Press, 2006); and "David Benatar, "The Misanthropic Argument for Anti-Natalism," in *Permissible Progeny?* eds. Sarah Hannan, Samantha Brennan, and Richard Vernon (New York: Oxford University Press, 2015), 34–64.

9. I first used this term in David Benatar and David Wasserman, *Debating Procreation: Is It Wrong to Reproduce?* (New York: Oxford University Press, 2015), 129–130.

10. There are exceptions, I noted, in which death does actually contribute terrestrial meaning to a life.

11. I use scare quotes because although it is common to speak of somebody *saving* somebody else's life, that is an overly optimistic description. One is, in fact, extending a life or delaying a death. This does not make it less noble.

12. See, for example, Ernest Becker, *The Denial of Death* (New York: Free Press Paperbacks, Simon & Schuster, 1973); Ajit Varki, "Human Uniqueness and the Denial of Death," *Nature* 460 (August 2009): 684. Such authors suggest that humans would not be able to cope without denial of death, but the claim is not that all people *literally* deny that they are going to die. (However, it is arguable that those who believe in an immortal soul do, in some sense, literally deny that they will die. They may not deny biological death—unless bodily resurrection counts as a denial of bodily death—but they do deny that a person's essence will die.) For a discussion on different ways of knowing that one is going to die, see Herman Tennessen, "Happiness Is for the Pigs," *Journal of Existentialism* 7 (Winter 1966/1967): 190–191.

BIBLIOGRAPHY

Adams, E.M. "The Meaning of Life," *International Journal for Philosophy of Religion* 51 (2002): 71–81.

Alcor Life Extension Foundation. "Cryonic Myths," http://www.alcor.org/cryomyths.html#myth2 (accessed January 4, 2014).

American Cancer Society. "Lifetime Risk of Developing or Dying from Cancer," http://www.cancer.org/cancer/cancerbasics/lifetime-probability-of-developing-or-dying-from-cancer (accessed October 2, 2013).

Andrews, Frank M., and Stephen B Withey. *Social Indicators of Well-Being: Americans' Perceptions of Life Quality* (New York: Plenum Press, 1976).

Ariely, Dan. *Predictably Irrational* (revised and expanded edition) (New York: Harper, 2009).

Ayer, A.J. *The Meaning of Life* (London: South Place Ethical Society, 1988).

Baier, Kurt. "The Meaning of Life," in *The Meaning of Life* (second edition), edited by E.D. Klemke (New York: Oxford University Press, 1999), 101–132.

Battin, Margaret Pabst. *Ethical Issues in Suicide* (Upper Saddle River, NJ: Prentice-Hall, 1995).

Baumeister, Roy, et al. "Bad Is Stronger Than Good," *Review of General Psychology* 5 (2001): 323–370.

Becker, Ernest. *The Denial of Death* (New York: Free Press Paperbacks, Simon & Schuster, 1973).

Beckett, Samuel. *Waiting for Godot: A Tragicomedy in Two Acts* (London: Faber and Faber, 1965 [1956]).

Belshaw, Christopher. *10 Good Questions about Life and Death* (Malden, MA: Blackwell, 2005).

Benatar, David. "Assisted Suicide, Voluntary Euthanasia, and the Right to Life," in *The Right to Life and the Value of Life: Orientations in Law, Politics and Ethics*, edited by Jon Yorke (Farnham, UK: Ashgate, 2010), 291–310.

Benatar, David. *Better Never to Have Been: The Harm of Coming into Existence* (Oxford, UK: Oxford University Press, 2006).

Benatar, David. "Forsaking Wisdom," *Philosophers' Magazine* (First Quarter 2016): 23–24.

Benatar, David. *Life, Death and Meaning* (Lanham, MD: Rowman & Littlefield, 2010 [2004]).

Benatar, David. "The Misanthropic Argument for Anti-Natalism," in *Permissible Progeny?: The Morality of Procreation and Parenting*, edited by Sarah Hannan, Samantha Brennan, and Richard Vernon (New York: Oxford University Press, 2015), 34–64.

Benatar, David. "Sexist Language: Alternatives to the Alternatives," *Public Affairs Quarterly* 19 (January 2005): 1–9.

Benatar, David. "Suicide: A Qualified Defense," in *The Metaphysics and Ethics of Death: New Essays*, edited by James Stacey Taylor (New York: Oxford University Press, 2013), 222–244.

Benatar, David, and Michael Benatar. "A Pain in the Fetus: Toward Ending Confusion about Fetal Pain," *Bioethics* 15 (2001): 57–76.

Benatar, David, and David Wasserman. *Debating Procreation* (New York: Oxford University Press, 2015).

Bradley, Ben. *Well-Being and Death* (New York: Oxford University Press, 2009).

Brison, Susan J. *Aftermath: Violence and the Remaking of a Self* (Princeton, NJ: Princeton University Press, 2002).

Brown, John. *The Life and Letters of John Brown, Liberator of Kansas, and Martyr of Virginia*, edited by F.B. Sanborn, https://archive.org/stream/lifeandlettersof00sanbrich/lifeandlettersof00sanbrich_djvu.txt (accessed April 19, 2015).

Brown, Jonathon D., and Keith A. Dutton. "Truth and Consequences: The Costs and Benefits of Accurate Self-Knowledge," *Personality and Social Psychology Bulletin* 21 (1995): 1288–1296.

Cabell, James Branch. *The Silver Stallion* (London: Tandem, 1971).

Campbell, Angus, Philip E. Converse, and Willard L. Rodgers. *The Quality of American Life* (New York: Russell Sage Foundation, 1976).

Camus, Albert. *The Myth of Sisyphus*, translated by Justin O'Brien (London: Penguin, 1975).

Cancer Research UK. "Lifetime Risk of Cancer," http://www.cancerresearchuk.org/cancer-info/cancerstats/incidence/risk/statistics-on-the-risk-of-developing-cancer (accessed October 6, 2013).

Carr, Archie. *So Excellent a Fishe: A Natural History of Sea Turtles* (Gainesville, FL: University of Florida Press, 2011 [1967]).

Cave, Stephen. *Immortality: The Quest to Live Forever and How It Drives Civilization* (New York: Crown Publishers, 2012).

Chang, Edward (ed.). *Optimism and Pessimism: Implications for Theory, Research and Practice* (Washington, DC: American Psychological Association, 2001).

Craig, William Lane. "The Absurdity of Life without God," in *The Meaning of Life* (second edition), edited by E.D. Klemke (New York: Oxford University Press, 1999), 40–56.

DeGrazia, David. "Is It Wrong to Impose the Harms of Human Life? A Reply to Benatar," *Theoretical Medicine and Bioethics* 31 (2010): 317–331.

de Grey, Aubrey. "Extrapolaholics Anonymous: Why Demographers' Rejections of a Huge Rise in Cohort Life Expectancy in This Century Are Overconfident," *Annals of the New York Academy of Sciences* 1067 (2006): 83–93.

de Grey, Aubrey, and Michael Rae. *Ending Aging: The Rejuvenation Breakthroughs That Could Reverse Human Aging in Our Lifetime* (New York: St Martin's Griffin, 2007).

de Unamuno, Miguel. *The Tragic Sense of Life* (London: Collins, Fontana Library, 1962).

Des Pres, Terrence. "Excremental Assault," in *Holocaust: Religious and Philosophical Perspectives*, edited by John K. Roth and Michael Berenbaum (New York: Paragon House, 1989), 203–220.

Easterlin, Richard A. "Explaining Happiness," *Proceedings of the National Academy of Sciences* 100 (September 16, 2003): 11176–11183.

Edwards, Paul. "The Meaning and Value of Life," in *The Meaning of Life* (second edition), edited by E.D. Klemke (New York: Oxford University Press, 1999), 133–152.

Ehrenreich, Barbara. *Bright-Sided: How the Relentless Promotion of Positive Thinking Has Undermined America* (New York: Henry Holt & Co., 2009).

Eliot, T.S. "Burnt Norton," in *Four Quartets*.

Epicurus. "Epicurus to Menoeceus," in *The Stoic and Epicurean Philosophers*, edited by Whitney J. Oates (New York: Random House, 1940).

Feinberg, Joel. *Harm to Others* (New York: Oxford University Press, 1984).

Feldman, Fred. *Confrontations with the Reaper: A Philosophical Study on the Nature and Value of Death* (New York: Oxford University Press, 1992).

Feldman, Fred. "Some Puzzles about the Evil of Death," *Philosophical Review* 100 (1991): 205–227.

Fischer, John Martin. "Why Immortality Is Not So Bad," *International Journal of Philosophical Studies* 2 (1994): 257–270.

Fischer, John Martin, and Benjamin Mitchell-Yellin. "Immortality and Boredom," *Journal of Ethics* 18 (2014): 353–372.

Frank, Arthur. *At the Will of the Body* (Boston: Houghton Mifflin Co., 1991).

Frankl, Viktor. *Man's Search for Meaning* (third edition) (New York: Simon & Schuster, 1984).

Franklin, Benjamin. "Letter to Jean Baptiste Le Roy, 13 November 1879," in *The Writings of Benjamin Franklin*, edited by Albert Henry Smyth, Vol. X (New York: Macmillan, 1907).

Frey, R.G. "Did Socrates Commit Suicide?" *Philosophy* 53 (1978): 106–108.

Gruman, Gerald. *A History of Ideas about the Prolongation of Life* (New York: Springer, 2013).

Hardcastle, Valerie Gray, and Rosalyn Walker. "Supporting Irrational Suicide," *Bioethics* 16 (2002): 425–438.

Hitchens, Christopher. *Mortality* (New York: Twelve, 2012).

Hume, David. "Of Suicide," in *Essays: Moral, Political and Literary* (revised edition), edited by Eugene F. Miller (Indianapolis, IN: Liberty Classics, 1987).

Inglehart, Ronald. *Culture Shift in Advanced Industrial Society* (Princeton, NJ: Princeton University Press, 1990).

Johansson, Jens. "When Do We Incur Mortal Harm?" in *The Cambridge Companion to Life and Death*, edited by Steven Luper (New York: Cambridge University Press, 2014), 149–164.

Joiner, Thomas. *Why People Die by Suicide* (Cambridge MA: Harvard University Press, 2005).

Judt, Tony. *The Memory Chalet* (New York: Penguin Press, 2010).

Kagan, Shelly. *Death* (New Haven, CT: Yale University Press, 2012).

Kahane, Guy. "Our Cosmic Insignificance," *Nous* 48 (2014): 745–772.

Kamm, Frances. *Morality, Mortality, Volume 1: Death and Whom to Save from It* (Oxford, UK: Oxford University Press, 1993).

Kaufman, Frederik. "Pre-Vital and Post-Mortem Non-Existence," *American Philosophical Quarterly* 36 (January 1999): 1–19.

Kripke, Saul. *Naming and Necessity* (Cambridge, MA: Harvard University Press, 1972).

Kurzweil, Raymond, and Terry Grossman. *Fantastic Voyage: Live Long Enough to Live Forever* (London: Rodale International Ltd, 2005).

Lamont, Julian. "A Solution to the Puzzle of When Death Harms Its Victims," *Australasian Journal of Philosophy* 76 (1998): 198–212.

Landau, Iddo. "Immorality and the Meaning of Life," *Journal of Value Inquiry* 45 (2011): 309–317.

Landau, Iddo. "The Meaning of Life *sub specie aeternitatis*," *Australasian Journal of Philosophy* 89 (December 2011): 727–745.

Law, Stephen. "The Meaning of Life," *Think* 11 (Spring 2012): 25–38.

Lax, Eric. *On Being Funny: Woody Allen and Comedy* (New York: Charter House, 1975).

Luper, Steven. "Death," in *Stanford Encyclopedia of Philosophy* (revised version), May 26, 2009, http://plato.stanford.edu/entries/death/ (accessed January 21, 2014).

Marshall, Patricia A. "Resilience and the Art of Living in Remission," in *Malignant: Medical Ethicists Confront Cancer*, edited by Rebecca Dresser (New York: Oxford University Press, 2012), 86–102.

Maslow, Abraham. *Motivation and Personality* (second edition) (New York: Harper & Row, 1970).

Matlin, Margaret W., and David J. Stang. *The Pollyanna Principle: Selectivity in Language, Memory, and Thought* (Cambridge, MA: Schenkman Pub. Co., 1978).

McGowan, Christopher. *The Raptor and the Lamb: Predators and Prey in the Living World* (New York: Henry Holt and Co., 1997).

McMahan, Jeff. "Death and the Value of Life," *Ethics* 99 (October 1988): 32–61.

McMahan, Jeff. *The Ethics of Killing* (New York: Oxford University Press, 2002).

Merkle, R.C. "The Technical Feasibility of Cryonics," *Medical Hypotheses* 39 (1992): 6–16.

Metz, Thaddeus. "Are Lives Worth Creating?" *Philosophical Papers* 40 (July 2011): 233–255.

Metz, Thaddeus. *Meaning in Life* (Oxford, UK: Oxford University Press, 2013).

Metz, Thaddeus. "The Meaning of Life," in *Oxford Bibliographies Online*, http://www.oxfordbibliographies.com/view/document/obo-9780195396577/obo-9780195396577-0070.xml (accessed June 9, 2010).

Miller, Henry. *The Wisdom of the Heart* (London: Editions Poetry London, 1947).

Myers, David G., and Ed Diener. "The Pursuit of Happiness," *Scientific American* (May 1996): 70–72.

Nagel, Thomas. "The Absurd," in *Mortal Questions* (Cambridge, MA: Cambridge University Press, 1979), 11–23.

Nagel, Thomas. "Death," in *Mortal Questions* (Cambridge, MA: Cambridge University Press, 1979), 1–10.

Neiman, Susan. "On Morality in the 21st Century," *Philosophy Bites* interview. March 27, 2010, http://philosophybites.com/2010/03/susan-neiman-on-morality-in-the-21st-century.html (accessed March 28, 2010).

Nozick, Robert. "Philosophy and the Meaning of Life," in *Philosophical Explanations* (Cambridge MA: Belknap, 1981), 571–650.

Oakley, Tim. "The Issue Is Meaninglessness," *Monist* 93 (2010): 106–122.

Parfit, Derek. *Reasons and Persons* (Oxford, UK: Clarendon Press, 1984).

PBS NewsHour. "As Humans and Computers Merge ... Immortality?" June 10, 2012, http://www.pbs.org/newshour/bb/business-july-dec12-immortal_07-10/ (accessed January 4, 2015).

Perrett, Roy. "Regarding Immortality," *Religious Studies* 22 (1986): 219–233.

Pitcher, George. "The Misfortunes of the Dead," *American Philosophical Quarterly* 21 (April 1984): 183–188.

Pizzo, Philip A. "Lessons in Pain Relief—A Personal Postgraduate Experience," *New England Journal of Medicine* 369 (September 19, 2013): 1092–1093.

Quinn, Philip L. "The Meaning of Life According to Christianity," in *The Meaning of Life* (second edition), edited by E.D. Klemke (New York: Oxford University Press, 1999), 57–64.

Rakoff, Ruth. *When My World Was Small* (Toronto: Random House Canada, 2010).

Rennie, John. "The Immortal Ambitions of Ray Kurzweil: A Review of Transcendent Man," *Scientific American* (February 5, 2011), http://www.scientificamerican.com/article/the-immortal-ambitions-of-ray-kurzweil/ (accessed January 4, 2015).

Santos, M.B., et al. "Assessing the Importance of Cephalopods in the Diets of Marine Mammals and Other Top Predators: Problems and Solutions," *Fisheries Research* 52 (2001): 121–139.

Scarre, Geoffrey. *Death* (Stocksfield, UK: Acumen, 2007).

Schopenhauer, Arthur. "Nachträge zur Lehre von der Nichtigkeit des Daseyns," in *Parerga und Paralipomena: Kleine philosophische Schriften*, Vol. 2 (Berlin: Hahn, 1851), 245–246.

Schopenhauer, Arthur. "On the Sufferings of the World," in *Complete Essays of Schopenhauer*, translated by T. Baily Saunders, Book 5 (New York: Wiley, 1942).

Shakespeare, William. *Macbeth*, Act 5, Scene 5.

Shapin, Steven, and Christopher Martyn. "How to Live Forever: Lessons of History," *British Medical Journal* 321 (December 23–30, 2000): 1580–1582.

Sinclair, Upton. *I, Candidate for Governor: And How I Got Licked* (Berkeley, CA: University of California Press, 1994).

Singer, Peter. *How Are We to Live?* (Amherst, NY: Prometheus Books, 1995).

Singer, Peter. *Practical Ethics* (third edition) (New York: Cambridge University Press, 2011).

Styron, William. *Darkness Visible: A Memoir of Madness* (New York: Random House, 1990).

Sumner, Wayne. *Welfare, Happiness, and Ethics* (Oxford, UK: Clarendon Press, 1996).

Swift, Jonathan. "A Voyage to Laputa," in *Gulliver's Travels and Other Writings*, edited by Ricardo Quintana (New York: Modern Library, 1958), 165–172.

Taylor, Richard. *Good and Evil* (Amherst, NY: Prometheus Books, 2000).

Taylor, Shelley E. *Positive Illusions: Creative Self-Deception and the Healthy Mind* (New York: Basic Books, 1989).

Taylor, Shelley, and Jonathon Brown. "Illusion and Well-Being: A Social Psychological Perspective on Mental Health," *Psychological Bulletin* 103 (1988): 193–210.

Teichman, Jenny. "Humanism and the Meaning of Life," *Ratio* 6 (December 1993): 155–164.

Tennessen, Herman. "Happiness Is for the Pigs," *Journal of Existentialism* 7 (Winter 1966/1967): 181–214.

Thomson, Garrett. *On the Meaning of Life* (Belmont, CA: Wadsworth, 2002).

Varki, Ajit. "Human Uniqueness and the Denial of Death," *Nature* 460 (August 2009): 684.

Walker, W. Richard, et al. "Autobiographical Memory: Unpleasantness Fades Faster Than Pleasantness over Time," *Applied Cognitive Psychology* 11 (1997): 399–413.

Walker, W. Richard, et al. "On the Emotions That Accompany Autobiographical Memories: Dysphoria Disrupts the Fading Affect Bias," *Cognition and Emotion* 17 (2003): 703–723.

Weiner, Jonathan. *Long for this World* (New York: HarperCollins, 2010).

Williams, Bernard. "The Makropulos Case: Reflections on the Tedium of Immortality," in *Problems of the Self* (Cambridge, UK: Cambridge University Press, 1973), 82–100.

Wolf, Susan. "Happiness and Meaning: Two Aspects of the Good Life," *Social Philosophy and Policy* 14 (1997): 207–225.

Wolf, Susan. *Meaning in Life and Why It Matters* (Princeton, NJ: Princeton University Press, 2010).

Wood, Joanne V. "What Is Social Comparison and How Should We Study It?" *Personality and Social Psychology Bulletin* 22 (1996): 520–537.

Zellner, W.W. *Countercultures: A Sociological Analysis* (New York: St. Martin's Press, 1995).

Zerjal, Tatiana, et al. "The Genetic Legacy of the Mongols," *American Journal of Human Genetics* 72 (2003): 717–721.

INDEX

absurdity, 14, 20–21, 54–55. *See also* meaninglessness
accommodation. *See* adaptation
Adam, 153, 240n17
adaptation, 68–70, 82, 226n10
adultery. *See* infidelity
afterlife, 7, 38–39, 98, 168, 220n8, 238n59
Allen, Woody, 149, 238n56
altruism, 38, 220n7
  misplaced, 204
Ambady, Nalini, 140
angst, 13, 50, 54, 63, 88, 139, 161, 164, 191–192, 209
animals, 20–21, 30, 47–51, 85, 88, 96, 137, 211
  compared with humans, 38, 44, 46, 104, 159–160, 175, 197, 198
  predicament of, 8–9, 42–44
  suffering of, 8, 42, 77, 216n8, 221n20, 222n32, 223n38
annihilation, 3, 94, 96, 117–118, 143
  account of death's badness, 102–110, 122–123, 130–135, 136, 202, 232–233nn9–11, 236n41, 237n48
  distinguished from biological death, 134–135, 202, 238nn57–58
  See also death; suicide

anti-natalism, 11, 122, 123, 127, 207, 216n9
anxiety. *See* angst
assault, 42, 76. *See also* rape
  excremental, 198, 244n20
atemporalism, 113
atheism, 44–45
atheists, 10, 35, 83, 136, 144, 220n6
Auschwitz, 61. *See also* Holocaust

backward causation, 112, 118
badness. *See* value
Baier, Kurt, 222nn26–27, 224n46
Beckett, Samuel, 200
Belshaw, Christopher, 59
Bendjelloul, Malik, 140
bereavement, 96, 108, 151, 178
Beth's death, 112–117
Brod, Max, 25–26
Brown, John, 95
Buddha, 30

Camus, Albert, 163
Cavalry Officer, 132
children, 11, 15, 29, 53, 64, 66, 73, 78, 131, 157, 160, 178, 199, 229–230n43
  gaining "immortality" through, 149, 152, 245n1